"Be–Attitudes"
For The Church

Keith Huttenlocker

WARNER PRESS
ANDERSON INDIANA

Printed in the United States of America

Contents

For my sons:
MARK and MARTY.
May they always love the church
the way their father does.

Preface

This is the book I had to write. It has been in the back of my mind probably since even before I acknowledged a call to the ministry over sixteen years ago. A lifetime spent in the church has privileged me to share in those glorious times written of by the psalmist, "Behold, how good and how pleasant it is for brethren to dwell together in unity" (Ps. 133:1). I am firmly convinced there is no fellowship in all the earth which can compare with that to be found within the church. However, I am familiar with the other side, too. I know the tragedy of "church trouble." Few things are worse; few things uglier.

Cords of love, bonds of peace scissored ruthlessly! Bitterness, guilt, and heartbreak behind the pulpit, in the pew and on both sides of the aisle! Sometimes we say, "Is it the work of the devil?" In our more charitable and objective moments we attribute it to "misunderstanding." And at such latter times we are close to the truth, certainly much closer than when we hurl charges of carnality back and forth across the trenches.

Oh, there is carnality all right. But did we ever stop to analyze why? Until we answer that question we'll continue tearing one another up, with little understanding about how we got into the mess or how we are going to get out of it. People, especially *God's people,* want to get along. Most of the time they do. But sometimes they don't. How needless the conflict, how costly the loss of precious souls and the golden opportunities.

Trace the trouble to its beginning point, and chances are you will see that someone was threatened. Not a physical threat—at least in most cases—but a threat to his self-esteem. A clash of opinions which threatened someone's autonomy. A word or act of disapproval which threatened someone's sense of acceptance. A failure that threatened someone's sense of achievement. In response to the threat, there was a reactionary declaration or act. Consequently, trouble erupted with threat precipitating counter threat. If the cycle continued, trouble became full blown. Obviously, the solution is to prevent either the original threat or the counter threat. Thus the chain of reaction is never begun, or is soon broken. Accord is maintained or restored.

I see pastors who are frustrated and hurt. I see good laymen who feel rejected and have left a church without constructive recourse. None of us can always be perfectly understood. We cannot always have fulfilling experiences. But we can hope to understand our emotions and the emotions of others when things misfire. It is no coincidence that the Master "when . . . reviled, reviled not again; when he suffered, he threatened not" (1 Peter 2:23). He understood, and attributed even his crucifixion to the ignorance of his adversaries.

Why are we so easily threatened? How can we avoid threatening others? The following pages represent a very modest attempt to answer those questions, toward the goal of a vital, dynamic, relevant church in every community.

1

The Pastor Sets the Pace

*Blessed is the church
whose pastor is an amber window,
for the whole congregation
will be bathed with sunshine.*

Like the sun's rays streaming through a stained-glass window, the pastor's personality colors the people in the pews. If his attitude is positive and his disposition warm, the congregation as a whole will take on the amber glow of contentment. If his spirit is dark and his temperament mean, the church will be overcast with a sullen haze. That his influence should be so profound is inescapable. By virtue of his very position he cannot be other than the key to his congregation's happiness or unhappiness.

To change the comparison, like the father of a family, the pastor sets the tenor of the church's atmosphere. If he is explosive, retaliatory, suspicious, judgmental, or authoritarian, eventually he will have that kind of congregation. If he is gentle and kind, slow to anger and plenteous in mercy; if he is moderate and democratic, trusting and fair, in time the whole church will take on his likeness.

Someone has said that after five years a pastor's problems are his own creation. The logic is valid, although the

7

timetable may be too advanced. A pastor's sins and neuroses, like those of any progenitor, are visited upon the third and fourth generations. A problem church today probably has been a problem church for years (at least off and on). In more cases than not the explanation is a pastor who several decades ago injured the fellowship by impropriety or indiscretion. Consequently, even the children's children have been infected with a distrust of preachers. And every succeeding pastor has to reap a little of the whirlwind sown by his distant predecessor.

But this can be changed! The way is for that present pastor to be an amber window, imperturbably streaming golden rays of love into every pew until the last dark shadow has vanished. It may take more than five years, but it can be done. It will not be done by a succession of short pastorates. Nor will it be accomplished by an autocrat whose Messianic-complex compels him to stay until every last "troublemaker" has been cremated or driven from the camp. One man—stout of heart, sound of mind, firm of purpose, and above all, permeated by Christ's love—can transform a disgruntled congregation into a vital church

A certain church had been torn asunder by a series of unfortunate incidents extending over several pastorates. Called to this scene was a man of wisdom and godly love. Although limited in formal training, he was gifted with a gentle manner which brought healing to troubled spirits. He pastored those people for twelve years, and when he left, the only fitting comment to be made regarding that congregation was, "Behold, how they love one another." His successor, received with open arms, inherited a tremendous wealth of goodwill which had been built up over those twelve years. What a difference one amber window can make!

8

What are we saying? Simply that the deeply happy church begins with a genuinely happy pastor. Let's not oversimplify what happiness is. It is not enough that the pastor be happy when he is preaching, or happy when he is playing golf, or happy because he got a raise in salary, or happy because the attendance was good last Sunday. This will not necessarily edify the complexion of his church. He will produce a happy church only if he is *at heart a happy man.*

This brings us to a discussion of the pastor's emotional stability. Few professions are inclined to be more trauma-producing than the pastoral ministry. During a friendly conversation, I suggested to our family physician that whenever I felt inclined to pity myself, I thought about the doctors. He replied with great sincerity and feeling, "That's funny, because when I feel that way, I think about you pastors." Who should know better than a doctor the toll the ministry has on a man?

The pastoral ministry is no place for the maladjusted. The man who comes to this calling needs a great deal of emotional balance, or as psychologists call it, ego strength. If he is not at heart a secure man, he will become increasingly an insecure pastor. The ministry is such that it seems to exploit every personality weakness. Whereas one might have a dozen hang-ups and still function quite well as an accountant or farmer, almost every bent in a minister's thinking will militate against his effectiveness. If his emotional security is impaired to any degree, this may precipitate a crisis in his church or make it impossible for him to survive a crisis arising from other causes.

The pastor who contributes to a well-balanced church is the one who survives very nicely in the heat of the kitchen. His poise preserves the peace, whereas a less composed pastor by his reaction might trigger a chain of reactions among the people. A divided church usually is but the extension of a pastor who got "all shook up." A peaceful church is but the expressed solitude of its pastor's soul. Pastors should be shock absorbers, not vibrators, when it comes to preserving "domestic tranquillity" within the congregation. A pastor who is easily threatened will be a vibrator. One who is not easily threatened will be a shock absorber.

Rev. Alonzo pastored several congregations, with trouble arising in each one. In his last charge he acted as chairman of the board of trustees. He refused to allow his youth director to conduct youth meetings without his presence, and even insisted on attending every meeting of the women's society. Underneath this strange mode of operation was an overwhelming sense of insecurity, the obsession, "they are out to get me." Inevitably his hyper-suspicion fractured many relationships in the congregation and indirectly led to his ouster. While this is an extreme example, it does illustrate the disaster which can result when a pastor begins to act out of fear, feeling that either his reputation or position is in jeopardy.

The secure pastor has confidence in himself, faith in God, and a great trust in God's people. Unlike the brother above, he is not always reading something into words said or things done by members of his congregation, particularly those who are influential. He is not jealous of those within his congregation who are as admired as he. He is not fearful of those whose power could be used to challenge his own. He does not interpret disagreement with his ideas, criticism of his sermon, or exclusion from a small group get-together as personal rejection.

The secure pastor does not have to be surprised by a birthday party every year or praised excessively in order to feel his ministry is appreciated. He is comfortable with his people. Because he is not up-tight, they relax when around him. A feeling is transmitted throughout the fellowship, "our pastor accepts us. We accept him."

We are indebted to Eric Berne for his concept that each man looks at himself with complimentary or uncomplimentary connotation and at the world in friendly or unfriendly terms. Thus, says Dr. Berne, one person may say, "I'm OK; the world is OK." Another may say, "I'm OK; the world is not OK." Still another may say, "I'm not OK; the world is OK." Finally, someone else may say, "I'm not OK; the world is not OK." In this language, it is absolutely essential that a pastor take the first approach. If he fails to believe in himself, he will forever be expecting dismissal. Failing to believe in the people he serves, he will be constantly dubious of their motives. Only confidence and trust insulate against threats. Only insulation from threat produces balance and stability.

Unfortunately, the ministry sometimes attracts men who are out to prove a point. In the vast majority of cases these men are not aware of their subtle motives. In their own minds, God has called them and, heroically, they must respond—whatever the sacrifice. Often these men make substantial contributions, and God is actually able to capitalize on their submerged desires. However, this sometimes is not the case, and congregations suffer. Happiness for such men ends right where their hidden agenda becomes thwarted. Sometimes, seeming superspiritual or unusually dedicated, they show a different side when the church does not meet their own psychological needs.

Pastor Willis had a saccharin-sweet personality and established quick rapport with everyone. However, both his personal life and his ministry were characterized by broken relationships. Back of the highly advertised humility and meekness was an apparent iron will to dominate.

11

Every relationship which necessitated an exchange of ideas was jeopardized by his compulsion to rule and reign. This eventually left him with but a small congregation of subservient people who more-or-less accepted him the only way he could experience acceptance: as utter sovereign of his domain. His call to the ministry had served to fill an emotional need in his life. It had given him a platform from which to give orders, and in the name of the Lord, at that. However, that same greed for power defeated his ministry and crippled his church.

The dynamic church will have a pastor who feels no compulsion to be boss. Oh, he will be a leader. He will be content with God's way of granting to every man a large degree of self-control. He will be eager not for his own place in the church, but for Christ's preeminence. He will stimulate—rather than stifle—creativity among his people. He will attract and employ the best minds amenable to Christ. He will delegate responsibility and recognize lines of authority. He will solicit advice and welcome constructive criticism. The administration of his church will be characterized by democracy and ethical practice. His people will think of themselves as his partners, not his puppets. This will make them happy.

A sense of equality is quickly revealed in a man's preaching. A pastor so inclined does not feel singularly called to tell the whole world everything that is wrong with it. Some men parade as fearless prophets, but inwardly they often are filled with resentment toward others and/or self-hate. The stable pastor has no desire to lord it over anyone in his preaching. He has no ax to grind. He does not feel it necessary to judge his people every Sunday morning and execute them every Sunday night, as the manner of some is. He more often says, "Let not your heart be troubled," than, "woe unto you, ye generation of vipers."

12

Ultimately, it is positive, uplifting preaching and tender, loving shepherding which nurtures best.

People are happiest when their self-worth is confirmed. If there be any incentive in righteousness, if there be any consolation in grace, if there be any hope in redemption, let the pastor affirm it both in his preaching and in his relationships with his people. In doing so he will surround himself with a happy church.

Occasionally a man is attracted to the ministry as a means of making a name for himself. The ministry still is an honored profession, and it does something for a man— some men, at least—to be called Reverend (better yet, Doctor). Chances are such men have a very low self-image and feel they need a high office to elevate them. (In reality, the man must elevate the office if the office is to elevate the man.)

Pastor Daryl started preaching when only a teen-ager. He was a fiery orator, preaching with a passion and caring deeply for individuals. Slowly he made his way up through the ranks of the unknown. His selfless service brought him prominence. Though still quite young, he was called to a fairly large church, then a still larger one. The big city church looked alluring, and so he moved again.

Now it seemed that he began to lust for prestige. He resembled less and less a lover of souls and more and more a shrewd businessman. Like a race driver trying madly to overtake the lead car, he pushed too hard and eventually spun out, losing control during temptation. However, long before the wreck he had ceased being a happy man and had become a man driven to prove he was the cream of the crop.

The secure church is pastored by a man whose personal aspirations are under close control. He has ambition, but he is not self-ambitious. He wants God's work to go for-

13

ward, but he doesn't care who gets the glory for it. He doesn't have to have a new building or the largest Sunday school in the state in order to validate his talent or bolster his sense of self-worth.

The relevant church is pastored by a man who makes his people mission minded, not for his own sake, but for Jesus' sake. The slave-driving pastor or the perfectionist makes everybody miserable in his frenzy to succeed. He is always berating somebody for not making him look good (though he doesn't state it that honestly). Not so with the pastor who knows that his calling is only to be faithful, and not necessarily to succeed. He has only to do his job—that in itself is his self-authentication. The results he leaves with God. The reward he leaves to eternity (those who strive only for fame have their reward in this world).

If and when success does come, the fulfilled pastor can handle it. He is delighted to share the honors. Yes, even to defer them. He sees himself as working together with his people, and indebted to them for much that he has accomplished. They, in turn, do not feel they are laboring to glorify a one-man show. They are happy to support a man who labors in humility. They rejoice when recognition comes to him, and in identifying with him, find their own sense of achievement.

Dr. Swan Haworth was one of my favorite professors. Before joining the seminary faculty, he pastored for twenty-five years, during which time he served but three churches. Every one of them was a happy church. Dr. Haworth remembers his pastoral ministry with great fondness. He was a successful pastor because he was a contented man. Throughout his ministry he furthered his education and shared the gleanings with his people. He not only loved them into Christ, he educated them into maturity. He was an amber window.

2

Problems: Opportunities in Disguise

*Blessed is the church
where there is understanding,
for every tie shall be secure.*

I was leading a small group discussion as part of a minister's inservice training program. "I have a problem," said a pastor, his face a study in earnestness. As you might guess, the problem involved a member of his congregation. He spoke of a middle-aged woman who over a number of years had allegedly terrorized each of his predecessors and was even now making life extremely difficult for him.

Nor was the woman's divisiveness confined to the local scene, for the pastor was particularly grieved over this woman's reported verbal attack on the leader of a recent Christian Education convention. "What can I do?" he asked despairingly. It was apparent that he already had made up his mind about what he was going to do, since he announced to us, "I'm going to leave." Within a few months he was gone, handing on the problem to his unenviable successor. That he left an unhappy church behind and that he left as an unhappy minister are obvious deductions.

Assuming this report was valid (and the man's reputation and record lead me to believe it was), this situation is typical of others and altogether unbecoming to any group purporting to represent Jesus Christ. Yet the question persists: What can be done?

Although they parade under a variety of guises (to protect the guilty), the great majority of church schisms stem from a clash of personalities. Usually these involve the pastor and one or more laymen in the church. In almost every instance, at least one of the personalities involved is maladjusted to some degree. As we saw in the preceding chapter, often the pastor is at fault. Because of his own hang-ups, he precipitates problems, or at least substantially contributes to them. By his own reactionary attitude, the pastor can aggravate a situation which would have passed without a ripple, had it been handled with discretion.

But let us be fair. Not all church problems are preacher-problems. In many cases, such as in the one above, trouble originates with a disturbed layman whose distorted view strains relationship after relationship, time after time, despite the exercise of patience and wisdom by the pastor. We shall not have happy churches until such a time as we acquire the means with which to cope with these inwardly wretched persons who chronically disrupt the peace of local congregations.

It is ironic that blatant displays of carnality should occur within the religious community. One would certainly not deny the hymnwriter's assertion that there is "power in the blood to save from sin, to bring the peace of God where guilt hath been," but experience tells us that many a man who claims to be "saved and sanctified" is nonetheless a genuine thorn in the side of his pastor and many other members in the church. Many people experience only partial conversion. They are like the blind man of Bethsaida who after Jesus' first touch said, "I see men as trees walking." Some people require the second touch of pastoral (and perhaps even medical) care if they are ever to be made whole.

I personally pastored for too many years before realizing that not all persons respond to the same treatment. Were it not for continuing education, I probably would not yet be aware of it. Psychologists tell us that there are approximately seven different personality types, each requiring a particular kind of care in order to stimulate the most effective relationship. A pastor needs to know whom to treat with firmness, whom he must shower with love and attention, whom he must allow to lean on him, and whom he must not allow to lean on him. He needs to know who will want to be approached cautiously and who will want an overt approach.

Lyle C. had been a backslider for years. He was in poor health and often in the hospital. Each time, he welcomed my prayers, but never came to church after being discharged. Finally, I said to him on one of my visits, "If I had as much wrong with me as you have, I wouldn't waste five minutes away from God." It worked! In two weeks Lyle was in church, and in a month he was converted. He has been an inspiring example to us ever since.

Armanda D. was elusive when she first started attending our church. Although pleasant, she would not permit better acquaintance. After she had come regularly for several weeks, I invited her to participate in a fellowship time for people new to our congregation. She declined and was absent the next three Sundays. I knew we had gotten too close. I did not pursue the contact. Finally, she phoned and asked to see me at once. I was not available, but returned her call as soon as possible. An appointment was made for later in the week.

Just as I expected, she phoned the day prior and cancelled her appointment. I did not push, but assured her of my continuing concern. The following Wednesday evening, she asked to see me at the close of prayer service. At that

17

time, she shared freely her problems and closed out the interview by inviting Christ to become her Savior. Two entirely different approaches to two entirely different types of personalities. That's one way to build a vital church.

Experience has indicated to me that two basic personality types necessitate the most pastoral care, both as to conservation and evangelism. These are: (1) The individual suffering from acute feelings of inferiority, and (2) the person who is hostile to all authority figures (including the pastor and perhaps even God). Both of these problems are rooted in childhood and constitute serious social handicaps to those suffering from them. Not infrequently both conditions reside in the same person. This is unfortunate, but not cause for despair. Because feelings of inadequacy and hostility are so common (both within and without the church), individual treatment will be given these subjects in succeeding chapters.

Inferiority and hostility are characterized by isolation, friction, self-contempt, anxiety, and grief. They keep some people from ever finding their place in the church. They cause others to drop out of the fellowship, sometimes even those who have been deeply involved participants for a number of years. Such feelings cannot work their social degradation without also taking their toll spiritually. Whatever jeopardizes a person's relationship with the church, ultimately threatens his relationship with God. Inferiority and hostility need to be exorcised like foul spirits so those plagued by them will at last be free to love and be loved.

The ultimate goal, deliverance, may take considerable time. Meanwhile, care should be taken to support those who are easily disturbed and to avoid trampling their sore spots.

The person who feels inferior should be given much praise and recognition. It should never be presumed that

18

he knows he is appreciated. Silence to him does not mean approval. It means disapproval. Failure to speak, failure to call, failure to applaud amounts to rejection. This person will need his successes maximized and his failures minimized. He should not be given some "big, important job" for which he is not qualified, in order to "make him feel important." He is apt to fail, consequently feeling more inferior than ever. And he will feel bitter toward the pastor, or whomever (as well he might), for having allowed him to make a fool of himself. Instead, he should be given the size task which he is capable of performing well and with which he feels confident. As he succeeds at little things, he can be given larger tasks. Thus will his confidence and competence grow.

It is not wise to openly disagree with the person who feels hostile toward authority figures. What sounds like constructive criticism to others, sounds to him like a reprimand. What sounds to others like a mild request, sounds to him like a demanding order. When speaking to or even in the presence of such a person, strong, opinionated statements should be avoided. He quickly "gets the number" of persons who speak thusly. They are to him just like the person(s) responsible for his hang-up.

It is best to ask the advice of those who feel hostile toward authority, rather than displaying too much initiative oneself. Such persons welcome inclusion on the leadership team, often accept and discharge responsibility very well, and are unusually loyal to the person who, by his democratic approach, bestows the equality they have often felt deprived them.

As a pastor, I have two reasons for wanting every member of my congregation to be happy. One is the shepherd's noble desire to care for his flock. The other is purely selfish: the unhappy person sows unhappiness wherever he goes—including in the church—and that adds to my job. Whether a person is unhappy because of maladjustment or because of a crisis which has temporarily made his life miserable, he is not easy to cope with, and woe unto the lamb who must feed beside him.

Obviously, in a church fellowship of any size there will be a few persons who suffer from the emotional complications mentioned above. Does this mean the conflict is unavoidable? Definitely not. A congregation can maintain balance despite the presence of disturbed persons. Indeed the church must not only accept such persons, but actually be involved in their therapy. (See chapter 5.) A local congregation can absorb a rather large number of distraught members, provided pastoral care and the maturity of fellow-members are adequate. Otherwise, however, one or two offenders may spark a conflagration which will spread throughout the fellowship.

As the church sails into the angry waters of interpersonal stress, the pastor is the prow. He must lead the way and meet the waves in such a way that it makes smooth, rather than turbulent, sailing. Here he will need a great share of the grace of God within his own soul. If he doesn't love people and sincerely want to help them, if he doesn't share Jesus' feeling that the sick more than the whole have need of a physician, he is in the wrong profession. Inevitably, he will be part of the problem instead of part of the solution.

A pastor must pray without ceasing to have compassion, not only for the multitude, but for that lonely figure who trudges to his study, or the one who cries out to him from behind the crowd, or the one who simply looks upon him longingly. Most of all, he should pray to have compassion for that one who despitefully uses him, recognizing that this one beyond all others is sending out SOS signals.

However, the pastor will need more than love. He must also have wisdom and knowledge. It is for him to facilitate the healing of those distressed-and-distressing members of his congregation. He is responsible, insofar as is humanly possible, to see that those unhappy people dotting the pews find happiness before they bring unhappiness to the entire congregation and/or great damage to themselves. His ministry, then, becomes, in effect, the salvation of his ministry. By restoring individuals, he preserves the group.

Hopefully, the pastor's training has equipped him for the task. Given sufficient psychological insight his administration of the church and informal contacts with members of the congregation will take into consideration the sore spots experience has identified. This will keep him out of a lot of trouble, and very legitimately win him much favor among those gratified by his warm friendship, a welcome contrast to the many unhappy associations they have experienced.

Not only will the pastor need to analyze personality idiosyncrasies, he will teach his people to identify them in themselves and in others, in each instance making allowance for them. In this way he best engenders forbearing attitudes. Usually he will not do this directly, such as saying, "Tom, you must overlook George's actions because he never resolved his Oedipus complex," but in a nonpersonal way point out why we all have the unwelcome feelings which on occasion we do.

A church which is educated in the ways of the human personality is able to live more peaceably with itself. Members not only understand their own peculiarities, they understand those of their brethren. They control their own behavior with greater efficiency, and forgive the errant behavior of others with greater ease.

Often the pastor's ministry to the troubled personality includes formal counseling (in difficult cases referral to a counselor with more advanced skills is recommended). Usually, members seek their pastor, but sometimes he must take the initiative. In the privacy of his study, pastor and layman can explore together the latter's inner unrest. Fears, resentments, complexes, and doubts are aired. An explanation for each is sought and frequently found. Armed with creative insights, the counselee goes forth to conquer his troublesome hang-ups. And often, with God's help, he is successful.

One by one, marriages are saved, parent-child relationships are improved, bitterness between in-laws is resolved, misunderstandings within the congregation are healed, and people begin to live the abundant life. Wherever you find these miracles taking place, there you will find an understanding church.

3

Ministry to the Over-Sensitive Person

> *Blessed is the church*
> *whose members know themselves,*
> *for great shall be her maturity.*

The beginning of all healthy relationships is proper respect for oneself. The reverse of this follows naturally: a poor attitude toward oneself will produce tension between oneself and others. Tragically, many people grow up with keen feelings of inferiority, both those of inadequacy and unworthiness. Because they are forever downing themselves inwardly, they often are heard downing others outwardly.

A number of factors can contribute to a deficiency of self-appreciation, ninety-nine percent of which date back to one's childhood and adolescence. The child who is criticized or rejected (overtly or covertly) by his parents or peer group almost certainly will feel inferior. So also may the child who grows up in extreme poverty, the child who faces discrimination day after day, the handicapped child, the child who is overmanaged (smothered), the child whose father or mother is alcoholic or immoral, the child whose parents are divorced, and the child who repeatedly is unfavorably compared with a sibling or other rival. While many of us are aware of our particular "disgrace," others are not. Some have never even identified the fact that they have a problem.

God wills that each of us hold a positive attitude toward himself. He values individual worth and wants us to do the same. Jesus taught, "Thou shalt love thy neighbor as thyself" (Matt. 19:19). Ordinarily we place the focal point of this scripture on the neighbor. The reference to "thyself" is even more important. Ponder this: You cannot love your neighbor more than you love yourself. Anything which limits love for yourself will in like measure limit love for another. The reason is very simple. Until you love yourself, you will be preoccupied with receiving love, and hence will give little heed to loving others. Until you feel your personal worth confirmed, you will be obsessed with accomplishing that feat, and hence will do little to help others confirm their worth. The person who does not love himself is just naturally a getter, not a giver. Far from being sinful, self-love is God-honoring. It is essential to spiritual victory and social compatability. Many of the unsightly self-displays which laymen view as expressions of carnal pride are not the result of too much self-love, but too little. They are but reactions to a humiliating sense of worthlessness.

There are at least twenty ways by which feelings of inferiority can stifle your quest for happiness and cause you to be a source of unhappiness to others.

1. Selfishness. Attention, service, praise, affection, possessions—these and many other things serve to build one's sense of self-importance. If you lack a sense of importance, you will more than likely be looking for things such as these for compensation. You won't like yourself for being selfish, but inwardly you will feel compelled to take and take and take, always under the illusion that being the center of attention proves you are somebody.

24

Hilda had a reputation among the women of the church for being selfish. Other men's wives would click their tongues and say, "Poor Gus. Hilda makes him do all the housework; she spends all his money on clothes for her back and she complains constantly about her health." Now, Hilda was not a bad person, not really. I rather liked her. It was just that she thought so poorly of herself that she made Gus try to convince her otherwise. Of course he was never able to do it. He probably didn't even realize what he was supposed to be doing.

2. Bullheadedness. If you think poorly of yourself, you never will be able to admit yourself wrong or mistaken. To do so would betray your closely guarded secret, namely, that you are not much. If one has no other claim to fame, he has to hang on to his omniscience. Always being right proves his importance. Harley never lost an argument. He always had a comeback. Neither did he have many friends in the church youth group.

3. Overbearing. Not everyone who thinks poorly of himself shrinks into the corner like a lamb. Some come out like a lion, determined to win friendship or adoration, thus justifying themselves. It was Edith's first time at the missionary circle meeting. She so dominated the scene that one would have thought her the senior member. Several of the girls "turned her off." They didn't realize she was only saying, "Look at me. I'm important too."

4. Withdrawal. Edith's opposite number is the person with whom you cannot make friends, no matter how hard you try. His or her attitude is, "Look, you really don't see anything desirable about me. Let's face it, I'm untouchable. Don't tempt me with your insincere friendship. I've been hurt enough already. Go away and let me be lonely in peace."

25

5. Overmotivation. The person who thinks poorly of himself may seek to recover by making himself a success —financially, socially, or professionally. Such people often are quite productive and achieve deserved preeminence in the secular world. However, when their lust for position is manifested in the church, it often precipitates jealousy and strife, even when service is well intended and efficiently rendered.

At the close of a prayer retreat, an elderly woman asked if she might speak to me privately. She proceeded to confess that she was fighting a real battle with resentment. It seems that a newcomer had rapidly usurped three of the most prestigious positions in the church, including one previously belonging to her. Reportedly this had been the other woman's pattern as she had moved from church to church. This being true, it would be an obvious case of someone trying to substantiate her significance by "showing her stuff." Having done so in any given place, there would be little left for her to do but repeat the act elsewhere. Moving would always be made easier by having irritated most of the church in her climb to the top.

6. Undermotivation. Here we have the reverse of the person described above. Underachievers are usually so convinced of their own futility that they simply don't try very hard to succeed. They are commonly thought of as lazy or limited. The truth is that in most instances all they need is a reason to believe in themselves. Gene has drifted from job to job, with long intervals of unemployment in between. Eventually his wife left him because he did not support her. Yet, Gene is a very winsome person. He has a minor handicap that has held him back. Somewhere back through the years he decided there was no overcoming it, and so he quit trying. We can't keep him in church because his failure complex even carries over to his religious life.

7. Arrogance. A well-known preacher tells of his surprise when a comment about him came back second-handedly, "That _____ doesn't need anybody." The reference was to his independent air. But the impression was not an honest one. "The fact is," said the minister, "I have a great need for other people. What people think has always been too important to me." Some people carry their inferiority as superiority. It is a subterfuge. By displaying an attitude just the opposite of the one really felt, they hope to direct attention away from their assumed inferiority. The person who implies he does not need the love of the rest of the church probably is the very one who feels most keenly its absence.

8. Braggadocio. Bragging operates on the same principle of deception as arrogance, only it is expressed in words rather than in bearing. In his much boasting, the braggart is only saying, "Since no one has a good word to say for me, I'll say it myself." In doing so, however, he isolates himself since even in the church, people resist the proud.

9. Detachment. Some of us, feeling insignificant, do not retreat into a shell. Nor do we bowl people over. Instead, we develop a sophisticated tactic that would seek some middle ground while still preserving the hang-up. Thus we associate freely and even impressively with the group. We are there, and we are not there. We enter into conversations, but we keep the talk trivial. We never reveal much of our hopes or fears, strengths or weaknesses, virtues or vices. We remain something of a mystery even to those who have known us for years. We are phantoms, if not phonies. Thus do we deprive ourselves of that intimate fellowship which makes church affiliation meaningful. We never feel close to anyone. We remain hidden because we feel that if our true selves were ever revealed, we would be rejected.

27

10. Easily offended. Alice and her husband had drifted from one church to another. She was barren, insecure, and unfulfilled. For the most part she had not related well to her pastors, but when a new minister came to the church, she made a bold and gracious bid for his friendship, and that of his family. For a time, theirs was a model relationship.

However, he did not comprehend the suspicion and feelings of unworthiness which beset her. Thoughtlessly, he stepped on the toes of her family's pride. Instantly, she and her household retreated in anger. When the pastor tried to make amends, she was defensive. She said, "We've been through this enough. If we can't get along with you, we'll just quit," and quit they did, rather than risk further hurt.

That person in the church who must be "handled with kid gloves" has a very poor self-image and is consequently offended by any remark or handling that tends to confirm his suspicion of being unwelcome or unappreciated. Sometimes those who feel rejected retaliate. At worst, it may mean an organized offensive to get rid of the pastor. At least, it may mean chronic criticism of the congregation's "in group." Once his feelings are hurt, the person affected will remain basically unhappy until consoled or time has healed his wounds. During the duration of his anger, nothing about the church will please him (except its failures). He will neither dance when piped to nor mourn when others weep.

11. Jealousy. The person who thinks poorly of himself resents those who excel him or who possess what he covets as a means to his own validation. The sight or mention of those who by comparison magnify his shortcomings is like waving a red flag. He will find it easy to speak ill of them, hard not to treat them coolly. Jealousy is a monkey wrench in the fellowship of the church.

28

12. Overdependency. There are at least two reasons why the person who feels inferior may resort to overdependency: (a) Having no confidence in himself, he is likely to feel helpless, looking to others for direction and assistance. (b) Needing to be the center of attraction, he may find it ego-boosting to have another act as his secretary of state. Such people really use their pastor. Pastors who need to be depended upon to bolster their own sense of self-worth respond readily to the overly dependent. They may succeed in carrying such persons along, but they never help them become whole persons, and when a pastoral change is made, the overly dependent person may find himself in a dilemma.

13. Overindependence. This is arrogance put into practice. Not every person who feels inferior confesses it by dependency. Some, instead, seek to deny it by their ultra-independency. They may help others within the church, but they want no help from anyone. Thus, in their own way they rob themselves of real fellowship, just as do the detached. The way to meaningful relationships in the church (as well as without) is neither through dependence or independence, but through *interdependence*. This means both giving and accepting help as occasions make each appropriate.

14. Gossip. We talk about people for one of two reasons: (a) by spreading derogatory information about them we hope to succeed in proving them as inferior as we ourselves feel, or (b) we expect to gain a friendship or two by being such a ready source of news. Whichever our objective, we are out of order and would not resort to such despicable tactics if we thought more highly of ourselves.

One day several women of our church were making candy in a room adjacent to our church office. Their chatter could be clearly distinguished from where the secretary sat at her desk. Our secretary, who is not a member of our congregation, observed something commendable about the conversation going on outside her door. She said, "They don't gossip." Hour after hour these women worked, talking constantly, but not once did any of them feel it necessary to court attention by gossiping.

15. Possessiveness. Inferiority is equated with being unlovable. Can you imagine, then, what it means to a person who feels inferior to find someone who genuinely does seem to love him? He must guard this love. He must squeeze it tight, lest it get away. He must seek its constant confirmation. He will repeatedly question its staying power. He will find rejection without cause. The person who feels inferior may, in his possessiveness, alienate himself from the few friends he has enjoyed in the church. This only adds to the sense of isolation and intensifies feelings of resentment and frustration.

16. Tightwad. "Since no one thinks well of me, I must look out for myself." So reasons an occasional person who lacks self-love. Not having a sense of belonging creates great insecurity, for it is in community that we all hope to survive. Most, if not all, of the people in the church who are poor stewards, suffer from feelings of inferiority, manifested as either selfishness or insecurity. They ask no quarter and give none. The reason: they are convinced it would do no good.

17. Do-gooding. The do-gooder feels quite the opposite of the tightwad. The do-gooder still has a few hopes. He believes it just may be possible to *earn* (dare I say, buy) a few friends by his generosity. Certainly this is not to say that all who are generous and helpful are neurotic. I am only pointing out that one of the ways by which some people hope to compensate for their inferiority is by making the church, as a whole or a few members, obligated to them. Elmira worked diligently for the church. When she

30

wasn't adequately praised, she left, saying, "No one appreciated me."

18. Vanity. One need not be a wicked witch to feel a compulsion to be the fairest of them all. All he or she may need is the impression that physical attractiveness is the key to popularity. If people have been accused of going to church to show off their clothes, the charge is not without foundation. But it isn't a healthy church if the object every Sunday seems to be to outdress the rest of the congregation. A beautiful spirit is more to be desired than fine clothes, yea much more than fancy wardrobes.

19. Lust. Lust is tragic in any fellowship. It is most unfortunate within the congregation of the righteous. Yet, occasionally there comes to the church circle one so destitute of love as to seek it at any level and at any price. Because love is more freely given within the fellowship of the church, it is only natural that those longing for it should seek it there. They become a problem, however, when they transgress moral boundaries. Moral laxity is a sign of desperation, a cue to the cheapness with which one views himself.

A fifteen-year-old girl, active in the church yet promiscuous, confessed to her pastor during a counseling session, "I have always felt so insignificant." Apparently feeling rejected by her mother, she gave herself to this boy and that one, looking for an acceptance she could not find.

20. Perfectionism. Perfectionism usually is admired, as well it should be. Yet slavish perfectionism indicates feelings of inferiority. Through perfection, the person who lacks self-acceptance hopes to attain a level of performance worthy of acceptance. Paul tried that as a Pharisee. The impossible demands of the law nearly drove him to insanity. Then he learned about grace. Thereafter, he said, "Not as though I had already attained, either were already, perfect: but I follow after" (Phil. 3:12).

31

The perfectionistic person will not have many friends, even in the church. He will be uncomfortable around people, and will make them uncomfortable around him. The perfectionist is always "up-tight" lest something embarrass him (that something being anything that would reveal his finitude). His preciseness harasses people. They feel that while around him they too must be perfect—think what this does to the perfectionist's children! They can't relax, be comfortable, or even human.

Ruby was a perfectionist. Her house was always immaculate. She was always perfectly groomed. Her family was always alerted to be on their toes to act properly. She was in many ways an unselfish, admirable person. Still when she headed up a department of the church's work there was constant controversy. Because she could not tolerate failure in herself, she pushed everyone else too hard.

Now, one should not be blind to the trouble he causes in the church. If he finds himself repeatedly resentful and creating resentments, he should look inwardly, not outwardly for the cause. The chances are very good that he will find that cause rooted in his own feelings of inferiority. An examination of his pattern of behavior is likely to reveal one or more of the traits covered in this chapter. As a professing Christian, he has no recourse but to confess his faults (yes, his sin) and to seek healing through repentance, counseling and other necessary means.

Recently, one of our most respected members told how for years he had suffered repeatedly from hurt feelings, and had responded in most petty ways to inadvertent injustices. Now he knows why that had been his practice. He still is sensitive (both God and the rest of us can forgive him for that), but he locates the blame as his own. He has learned to act responsibly. As such he helps all of us to "keep the unity of the Spirit in the bond of peace."

4

From Rebellious to Restored

*Blessed is the church
when individuals' needs are met,
for she shall be strong and fruitful.*

No single personality type poses more of a hazard to the harmony of a local congregation than does the person hostile toward authority figures. Because of his obsessive fear of domination, he will be threatened by the pastor's power at the slightest provocation. Because of his compulsion to demonstrate that he is no longer dominated (as in childhood), the individual hostile toward authority may from time to time test and even challenge the position of the pastor.

There usually is great strength in the person allergic to the power of others. It has been painstakingly developed over a number of years as the result of a life-style that has chosen to meet force with force. It has been his mode of survival. Ironically, in his quarrel with demagoguery the person who resents authority frequently becomes a demagogue himself. He covets the very power which has abused him. He wins it and then turns it on others.

The individual who is hostile toward authority is, in fact, a frustrated king. Were it possible, he would become a monarch, and thus by his absolute authority, eliminate all other sources of power, forever ridding himself of the fear of domination. This, of course, is the height of folly. Even those who have succeeded in gaining a monopoly on power have been plagued by the fear of being deposed. Herod and Caesar, of course, are classic examples.

There is a god-almightiness about those hostile to authority. It has had to come to that since even God, the ultimate Authority, has to be equalled or surpassed to put all authority beneath rather than above such people.

Aaron C. was such a person. Rather capable, quite personable and very dedicated, he had over the years been involved in several devastating schisms within his local congregation. He was, in fact, the center of each storm. When unthreatened, he could be magnaminous and witty. However, whenever it appeared that the power of the church was slipping out of his hands and into the hands of the pastor, he became anxious. So far as creation in his local church was concerned, "all things were made by him; and without him was not anything made that was made." Thus John's reference to Christ's role in creation (John 1:3) suggests that in this fellow's church, if the pastor wanted to get a program through, it first had to be approved by him. Many people in the church thoroughly believed in him. Others, quite naturally, feared him and blamed him for the unhappiness which had recurrently plagued the congregation through the years.

Of course, such persons as the one described above are commonly referred to as the "church boss." There was a time when it seemed there was one in every congregation. There still are bosses in many, particularly among smaller churches (that's the primary reason they are still small). Mark it down: the church boss is hostile toward authority. That's how he got his office. He is the resident demagogue. The pastor may be a demagogue, too. However, he is the guest demagogue. If the two take up arms against each other, one will become demagogue emeritus.

During the era when the pattern of the local church called for the pastor to be a paternal figure, dominant in authority with few boards and councils to which he was accountable, the church boss was almost a necessary evil. The pastor's raw authority brought the blood rushing to the brain of the person hostile to authority. He was either self-appointed or chosen by consensus from among other less brave dissidents. He was to be the fire in the pew to fight the fire in the pulpit.

With the coming of more representative church government, the would-be church boss may now lack a cause. While deprived of the fulfillment of a knock-down-drag-out battle with the pastor (which had great therapeutic value as an outlet for hostilities toward any number of other persons), the church boss is placated by the fact that now he is not so often threatened by the prospect of domination. Of course those annoyed by authority figures can have trouble with other members of the congregation (particularly those of their own stripe) as well as with the pastor.

It is not hard to identify the person who is hostile toward authority. He is the one who thrives on arguments with anyone "in the know." He himself is an authority on almost everything. If you say, "It is a nice day," he says, "Looks like rain to me." He is the one who if offered a favor will decline, no matter how badly he needs it. He is the one—this is a dead giveaway—who orders his children around like he were a drill sergeant and they were new recruits.

Unfortunately, the points at which the pastor and the person hostile toward authority come to confrontation are numerous. To begin with, the person who dislikes authority figures will bristle at strong preaching. Even if he does not know the speaker, he will peg him, usually subconsciously, as "just like my old man." Even if the preacher is unaware of his presence in the congregation, the authority rejecter is apt to feel he is the direct object of each sermon. Every loud voice to him is intimidating (it brings back memories of childhood and home).

Ah, the board meeting. Look out! Put the authority figure on the Board of Trustees and he may become a terror. The first order of day will be to show the preacher who is running this ship. Well, maybe he isn't quite that bad, but don't cross him. Don't put down his ideas. Don't push too hard for programs about which he is dubious.

Whereas the person who suffers from an inferiority complex will take it hard if he loses an election, the person who suffers from an authority figure complex will take it hard if he loses an issue. The former will need to win at the polls to reassure him of his acceptance. The latter will need to win at the conference table to reassure him of his independence. One says to the pastoral leadership of the congregation, "Don't pass me by." The other says, "Don't push me."

The pastor is inevitably destined to encounter both as he travels the administrative highway. Hopefully, he will be able to avoid a fatal accident. (The life he saves may be his own.) Whatever problem he may pose, the person resentful of authority may very likely have much to contribute if properly cultivated. His leadership can as well be put to work for the pastor as against him.

This would be a good place to address a word (three will be enough) to young men considering the associate pastorate as a beginning place for their ministry. If you have an aversion to authority figures, *Don't do it!* The very necessary ascendency over you which the senior minister must exercise will irritate you no end and render your working relationship null and void. If you need to be number one all the time, there is some doubt about whether you should be in the ministry. Certainly, temperamentally you are unsuited to be the second man of a church staff. If you style yourself as a "strong leader," get out there in front where you belong and lead from an appropriate position.

Senior ministers also have a lesson to learn here. Those ministers who are insecure in their leadership probably should not become involved in a multi-staff ministry. They will be threatened by any assertiveness by an associate, particularly if he is capable and ambitious (even within limits of propriety). The fear that "He is going to take my place" will constantly gnaw away at the base of security.

Some senior ministers, needing the prestige of an associate, have found a way to have one without being threatened. They get themselves a "boy." He may be mature in years, but his primary requisite in making job application is that he aspire to being no more than an errand boy. If a bona fide leader finds himself playing "boy," his dignity suffers greatly. There is either a struggle for power or a quick exit by the associate. It is not hard to figure out that the pastor who is fearful of his associate's power is, himself, a person who lusts for power.

Meanwhile, back in the pew, not everyone who has a chip on his shoulder about authority will stay and fight when that chip is knocked off. Those of weaker nature simply will flee the presence of the authority, hurling a few well chosen barbs about or to him as they fade from sight. No conscientious pastor can feel other than badly when this happens. If he has any compassion at all, he inevitably will assume some of the blame.

While the departure of the offended leaves the pastor saddled with guilt feelings, it portends no more gladness for the departed. They will either drop out of church entirely, nursing their grudge to the detriment of both soul and body, or transfer their allegiance to another congregation, where the cycle of encounter and retreat is likely to repeat itself.

Many people now of the age normally more supportive of the church grew up in an era of totalitarianism. They were raised in homes where the father was a dominant, sometimes brutally forceful, figure. It is, of course, this father image which serves as the basis for all hostility toward authority (it can just as well be a mother image, and in some cases is).

Almost common is the man, say fifty years of age or older, who has spent the last thirty or more years being defensive toward persons in positions of authority. Typically, such a person was victimized by social and/or religious intolerance which robbed him of self-expression and cheated him of individuality. Legions of these have long since left the church, characteristically about the time they married, went into military service, or left for college (that was the day father lost his franchise).

Many of those who remain in the church are, as we have suggested, recurrently disruptive forces. If not overly troublesome, they often take the minority opinion on most issues (with no small amount of pride) and resort to at least passive resistance if they think they are being bulldozed. Incidentally, the more aggressive of such persons may make great union leaders since their choicest diet is a concession from the power structure. Conversely, when such persons attain position in management, they become the most belligerent union opposers.

We now have on the way a new generation raised on permissiveness (a swing of the pendulum from the era of totalitarianism). As we are already so painfully and vividly evidencing, this generation also has a problem with authority and poses a problem for persons in authority. Today's youth, subjected only to permissiveness at home, are ill-prepared for the restraints of adult society. They are like an untrained bronco, ready to throw the first rider. At first indication it appears the reaction of this generation to the authority of the church is that of avoidance. Many youth reject the church because they view its discipline as oppressive. If this generation comes into the church in later years, still angry at authority, we shall have more trouble than with those who grew up under too tight control.

Perhaps the most pathetic of all those who have problems with authority figures are those who feel ambivalence. It is not easy for a child to hate a domineering parent. Doing so carries with it the penalty of self-condemnation. And so some children both hate and love (if not simultaneously, with alternating current) the parent who dominates them. If neither submission nor rebellion (healthy forbearance is the desired response) has won by the time the child reaches maturity, his attitude toward all authority figures will be hate-love. He will find it impossible to adjust to those who exercise control over him. One moment he will want to pay them obeisance and the next moment he will want to fight them. He will be like the demoniac who, when approached by Jesus, asked Jesus to leave him alone and yet ran to fall at Jesus' feet.

I recall an obese, unattractive young woman who was a patient on my ward at the state hospital. Some days when I made my rounds she approached me with adulation. She could not say enough complimentary things about me and would use those phrases so expected of a model, ten-year-old Sunday school girl (whose manner she copied perfectly). Other days, however, the moment I entered the floor she might rush at me and order me off, cursing violently. She would say, "I don't want any _____ preacher telling me what to do." You get the picture: One day she welcomed authority. The next she struck out at it blindly.

We have persons like that in our churches (although, thank God, they usually are more subdued). That's why perplexed pastors can never understand why one day they are so popular and the next so unpopular. One young lady told me that for years she had alternately loved and hated her mother. Not surprisingly, she felt a similar ambivalence toward me. It was very helpful to both of us when we could talk about this. She became one of my valued friends.

Unfortunately, the majority of those who have ill feelings toward their pastor will not talk to him about it. The last time they talked to an authority figure about their feelings, dad (or mom) took them to the woodshed (literally or verbally). In fact, one of the reasons they are so steamed up is their frustration, their desire to be conciliatory, and their fear of making the first overture.

Jesus offered some counsel to those in conflict, which, if taken, would forestall many an impending misunderstanding and subsequent fracus: ". . . if thou bring thy gift to the altar, and there rememberest that thy brother hath ought against thee; leave there thy gift before the altar, and go thy way; first be reconciled to thy brother, and then come and offer thy gift" (Matt. 5:23-24).

In the rebellion-free church there will be dialogue. Both the pastor and the person allergic to authority will be open enough to talk about the problem between them, such openness being born of evidence that each is reasonable when given an honest opportunity to discuss differences.

5

"Little Christs"

*Blessed is the church
whose members minister to each other,
for the weak shall be made strong.*

Luther said, "We are to be little Christs one to the other." This thought, of course, is close to the essence of Protestantism. The concept of the "priesthood of all believers" has even greater implications than generally given to it. It does include the individual's right (and responsibility) to search the Scriptures for himself. It also includes his right to petition God directly without need of any mediator except Jesus Christ.

Moreover, however, the priesthood of all believers recognizes the ministry of believers to believers. This does not preclude the role of the pastor. Rather, it supplements and is vital to the support of the pastoral function. Indeed, part of the pastor's ministry is to teach his people how to minister to each other, how to be little Christs. This is spelled out clearly in Ephesians 4 where Paul says that God gave "some pastors . . . to build up the body of Christ" (v. 12).

More and more the world recognizes the ministry of interpersonal groups. It is generally agreed that great work is being done today among alcoholics by Alcoholics Anonymous. The heart and soul of the AA approach is

41

member boosting member. Likewise, the psychologist knows that he can take a patient just so far via the counseling process. Eventually the patient will need to move into group therapy, where in intimate communication with other troubled persons he will discover his true self as revealed through the eyes of others.

Long ago Jesus envisioned a great clinic of the soul (and mind). He said, "I will build my church." To this day no other group holds such re-creative possibilities as does the church. For the recovery of sin God presents his redemptive team: the Savior, the pastor, and the church. Though the church is not the greatest of these, its significance cannot be overlooked.

The New Testament is replete with references to the ministry of believers to believers. "Look out for each other's interests, not just for your own" (Phil. 2:4, TEV). "Wherefore comfort one another" (1 Thess. 4:18). "Teaching and admonishing one another in psalms and hymns and spiritual songs" (Col. 3:16). "Consider one another to provoke unto love and good works: exhorting one another" (Heb. 10:24-25). That congregation, peopled with little Christs who edify one another, cannot be other than a strong church. The quality of soul-care will make it so.

Those who think of the church as only a place where God is worshiped, or of a congregation as only those people with whom God is worshiped, miss the mark. This is as much a misconception as to say college education amounts only to what is experienced in the classroom. College education would not be complete without a student's having a dormitory roommate, walking to class with a friend, cheering in the grandstands with the rest of the student body, participating in a rap session while drinking Coke at the student union, going with one's date or spouse to the musical.

Nor is church membership to be equated entirely with what happens between 10:30 A.M. and 11:30 A.M. on Sunday morning. *Affiliation with the church is meaningless apart from social exchange.* The ministering church has a sense of entity that lasts the week long. Christ-centered conversations in the narthex, on the church parking lot, and over the telephone afford a continuing ministry. So does the togetherness of the women's society, the men's fellowship, the class party, the youth group, the visitation task force, and other intrachurch contingents. The happy church thrives on contact. That contact touches off *dynamic fellowship* which both preserves and promotes the individual believer's life in the kingdom.

No one knows better than God the creative power of fellowship. While it is true that people may never be worse than when together, it is equally true that they may never be better than when together. Compare the Charles Manson type commune with that New Testament community written of in Acts 2. While the children of darkness incite one another to riot, let the children of light incite one another to righteousness.

The ministry of believers to believers often is a very subtle matter. Contrary to a pastor's ministry, which of necessity is weighted toward preaching, teaching, or counseling, the ministry of believers is most typically informal, taking place in various manners in unscheduled places. In fact, for the most part, it is most effective when least obvious. Though this ministry usually cannot be structured, it does lend itself to classification.

There is the ministry of support. This includes any action which sustains a person in need of reserves beyond his own measure. Members of the church need long hems on their garments. This is to say that within any fellowship at any given time there likely will be those who are reaching out for help (overtly or covertly). These persons may

43

be going through deep trial, experiencing discouragement, or facing a great challenge. They require "virtue," or strength from those in the church who skirt them weekly. Within the helpful church there will be a number of concerned, sensitive individuals whose radar seems to receive distress signals from those nearby. Paul reminds us, "Bear ye one another's burdens, and so fulfill the law of Christ" (Gal. 6:2).

Promising to remember a troubled person in prayer can be a most effective means of support, provided it is not just a cheap way of discharging responsibility to him. At other times, taking a few minutes to listen may be just what is needed. Sometimes an appropriate verse from scripture or sharing a fitting personal experience brings meaningful support. Occasionally it may be possible to become involved in the person's dilemma and participate in effecting a solution.

Strong is the church where there are those skilled in getting the bruised to an inn, or quick to give a cup of cold water in the Master's name. In the ministering church the right hand of fellowship means more than token acceptance. It is a compact, a pledge of support when days are dark. No hand is worth giving unless it is dedicated to the well-being of the one receiving it.

There came to our congregation several years ago a young lady who suffers from myopia in one eye. Because of this handicap and a series of health crises experienced while very young, this woman suffered from an excruciating inferiority complex. Not only did this retard her social development, but over the years it had produced a depressed personality. At times her periods of despondency were frightening. But things began to change as this winsome, fragile soul entered into the fellowship of our congregation. For her feelings of inadequacy she found love, respect, and opportunities to contribute. During those tides of depression which swept over her with decreasing frequency she was surrounded by uplifting associations, particularly within a Tuesday morning prayer group.

The steady transformation in this young woman's life continues even to this day. She has not fully conquered, but she has come a long, long way. The Holy Spirit has been her constant comfort. Her pastor's teaching and counseling have assisted. However, the support of the church has made the vital difference.

Not all support relates to adversity. It can as well mean a word of praise during the calm as a word of comfort during the storm. The young lady just mentioned had published a book of poems. In this instance it was a case of "rejoicing with those who rejoice." We were all justifiably proud of her and praised her accomplishment. Many a man or woman can testify to the fact that he or she is in the church today because many years ago some thoughtful, gracious person praised some performance by the subject or made him or her feel welcome as part of the fellowship.

There is the sounding board ministry. This is for good listeners only. Here the technique is to let someone else bounce his thoughts off you, thoughts which he may think are weird, carnal, or heretical. These are thoughts usually difficult to share, and they are shared with only a few select, trusted confidants. The relevant church always has several such priceless persons. To them has been given the special knack of listening with composure and responding with restraint.

The sounding board ministry is especially effective to those who must ventilate their anger or pain because of offenses related to their feelings of inferiority or hostility toward authority. These people need someone to listen to them. Certainly not someone to agree with their bias or offer sympathy when sympathy is not justified. Neither, someone who will be reactionary and condemnatory.

What *is* needed is someone to listen patiently and sincerely, someone who will give every indication of hearing, but no indication of his own feelings about what has been said. The offended person usually doesn't want agreement or disagreement. He merely wants someone to know he has been hurt. Just feeling that someone understands and cares will in most instances be sufficient.

There is an old saying about the church custodian being the pastor's confessor. I once served on the staff with a good Christian brother who gladly assumed this role. There were Monday mornings when I poured out to him the frustrations I had taken to bed with me on Sunday night. He listened sympathetically, even if he couldn't compound any solutions. Having gotten it off my chest we both went about our business for the day in the joy of the Lord. (Conversely, there were other times when I served as his confessor.)

Fears, as well as hostility, open the door for a sounding board ministry. I once knew a sick, very old man. His case was terminal, although he did not know it. We had discussed spiritual matters and he had assured me of his right standing with God. Several times I encouraged him to talk about death, but he did not take his cue. Though he was not actually a member of our congregation I visited him in the hospital regularly. I was the only pastor he had.

One afternoon when it was late and I was in a hurry the opportunity came. I had asked how he was feeling. It was obvious he was very low. He replied, "I'm not feelin' so good today." Then he quickly changed the subject, for he never liked to complain. "How's the weather out there?" he asked, making a halfhearted effort to direct his gaze out the window.

"It is a nice day," I said. And then on a wild hunch it might lead to deeper things, I continued, "It will be spring one of these days."

"Yeah," he answered dubiously, "I just hope I'm around when it comes."

There was my chance! "You sound as though you have some doubts about it," I volunteered.

"I do," he replied wistfully. What followed was an honest and open conversation about the reality of death. To the best of my knowledge no one else had been able to allow him to get this load off his chest. His doctor had not told him the severity of his illness. It was my responsibility to listen to his fears. Any understanding Christian might have done the same, however.

Finally, doubts are served by a sounding board ministry. How else shall we come to faith if we do not cope with doubt? And how shall we answer doubt except to prick the minds of others? In the mature church there will be no penalty for sharing one's uncertainty about that which should be held with certainty. Honest doubt is not to be despised, but discussed—in a reasonable, emphathetic fashion. During a Sunday school class session one morning a youth admitted to having some question in his own mind whether there was a God. He complained later that the teacher and other students pounced on him so vociferously that he spent the next two years defending atheism, a position he had not originally espoused. Those in the understanding church will know better than to make this mistake.

Talking helps. It helps to clear our thinking. It expels poison. It strengthens resolves. It separates fact from fantasy. It negotiates peace or organizes for war.

Writing of the constructive interchange which should take place within the fellowship of the church, Sam Shoemaker stated, "Here partial or distorted or even completely false ideas can come out, and find corrective—not from a leader declaring in dogmatic fashion what the truth is, but from the speaker feeling always freedom to say what

47

he thinks, but then to hear also what others think. This double experience, of feeling that the group is going somewhere, and yet has time for the mistakes and even at times the garrulousness of a newcomer, may work off more mental and emotional tie-ups in people concerning religion than reading a hundred books and listening to a thousand sermons."[1]

There is the ministry of tutoring. This is the ministry of instruction and correction in righteousness. This is a very delicate ministry, but whatever its peril, it is essential if infants in the faith are to move toward the stature of the fullness of Christ, and if those who have begun to drift are to be restored. Here the group plays a crucial role. Some, but not all changes can be wrought from the pulpit or podium. There is no substitute for the influence of one's own peer group, in this case, laymen speaking to laymen.

Once again those who are hostile enter our discussion. Let us suppose, after a normal amount of ventilation, a person continues to speak resentfully of the pastor or others of the church. Let us suppose that his wrath does not cool within a reasonable length of time, that there is considerable evidence of a carnal spirit. It then becomes the responsibility of the one with whom this malice is shared to call it to the attention of the hostile person.

Perhaps a question will be enough, "Are you sure you are in control of your attitude about this?" If this is not enough, a more direct statement can be made, "I hear you saying that you have become embittered about this." The tone of voice and inflections will be crucial to the success of such intervention. The Bible refers to this action as "speaking the truth in love" (Eph. 4:15).

There are other times when a bit of gentle coaching is in order. Without apology the religious community should clarify the group norm. Only by so doing does it serve its members. This is a vital part of Christian nurture. The gentle persuasion of those who care for us as their own flesh is a rod and staff of comfort when we distrust our own will to do good. The solicitous concern of the sponsoring body is our security when the world threatens to beguile us of our reward. One of the greatest pastors I know says that he remained faithful as a young Christian simply because the church strengthened him. The admonition of a friend who sticks closer than a brother is an exercise in the spirit, not of the letter of the law.

Ultimately, however, the church tutors best by example. Inspiration is better than correction when it comes to "perfecting the saints." It is only natural that we should want to please those we love. This is where mere organization fails in gaining compliance from its members.

There came to one of the congregations I served a very teachable man who was keenly interested in our message. He was searching for abundant life. Sunday after Sunday he listened intently to my sermons. He enjoyed his Sunday school class where, amid many vital discussions, views were set forth which were much more stringent than those of his background. One day I received a note from him. It said—

Dear Reverend:

I will be attending a luncheon meeting today at which there will be drinking. Since our church does not believe in this, I felt I should tell you I probably will partake.

I never discussed the matter with him. I didn't have to. The little Christs had gotten through. He was already persuaded of the course he must eventually take. Take it he soon did, and for the remainder of my ministry to him and his family he continued as an abstainer.

Mature is the church where believers take seriously their priesthood.

---

[1]Samuel M. Shoemaker, *With the Holy Spirit and With Fire* (New York: Harper and Row, 1960), p. 112.

6

The Fellowship:
Unhealthy Versus Healthy

Blessed is the church
whose ministry is dynamic and adaptive,
for it shall not lack opportunities to serve.

A young man wrote to me saying he was enrolling that fall in college and would study for the ministry. I was very pleased to hear this. I was also momentarily startled, since I remembered the young man as but a small child in my first pastorate. The letter continued with news about the church. It read, "You've probably heard that we have a new pastor at home. He is very good, and he really lays it on the line." Now, I was bothered a little, for that reference to laying it on the line had a disturbing connotation to me. Unwittingly, the young man may have put his finger on the reason for many church crises.

Whatever the constructive ministry of the evangelist as a voice crying in the wilderness, congregations eventually wither under the constant onslaught of harsh denunciation. The damage is not to be measured in numerical losses alone. That good people should find it necessary to seek elsewhere for the message, "Come unto me all ye that labor and are heavy laden," is indeed sad.

What happens to the good people who remain is even more regrettable. They often become as negative as their pastor. Visitors sense the hostile atmosphere and usually do not return. If newcomers are attracted to this environment, they are likely to be disgruntles from other congregations or sourdough converts who have acquired a rigid piety. Young people feel oppressed and drop out at the earliest opportunity. Meanwhile, the self-righteous, ever shrinking group clicks its collective tongue and bemoans the evil and indifference of the modern world.

By the process of elimination and selective recruitment, the congregation takes on an undesirable character. It becomes, in fact, a neurotic fellowship, with paranoid policies and delusions of grandeur. Naturally, as with a neurotic person, there is much internal unrest and unhappiness. Let us compare the characteristics of a neurotic fellowship with those of a healthy fellowship.

Exclusivism vs Magnanimity

In order for neuroticism to be the pattern for a congregation, exclusivism has to prevail. When all or nearly all healthy elements (persons) have been expelled, there is little chance for the fellowship to regain its health. Exclusivism becomes entrenched.

The group views itself pharisaically. Self-righteousness justifies the isolation from individual Christians outside the group and the larger community of Christian churches. The apologetic is, "We are the only ones upholding the standard." A minister describes how it was in the congregation with which he was associated as a teen-ager: "Our pastor told us that our sister churches throughout the state had apostatized. Our national leaders were all sold out to Satan. Most neighboring pastors had compromised—a terrible word. I believed it and was sick about it. I felt so

51

cut off from the church at large, felt the cause of Christ was in serious trouble."

He continued, "Then I began to meet those from other congregations—largely against our pastor's wishes. The better I grew to know them, the more I respected them. I became acquainted with other ministers and I could tell they were not backsliders or heretics. Eventually, I bolted my home church and went where the pastor and the people recognized there were other Christians besides themselves. It turned out to be one of the best things I ever did, even though the people from whom I fled expected it to be my ruin."

In the healthy fellowship newcomers are welcome and their contributions are incorporated into the life of the church. There is a healthy respect for other groups. It is not a naive acceptance of anything and everything, but an appreciation for the fact that the last word rests with God and not with us. The healthy fellowship respects Christ's words, "Other sheep have I which are not of this fold," and shares his dream of "one fold, and one shepherd" (John 10:16).

Judgmentalism vs Charity

Not only is the neurotic fellowship ingrown, it is usually also very judgmental. Someone has said, "There are only two classes of people, the righteous and the unrighteous. And the righteous do all the classifying." At least this is the way it would seem in the neurotic fellowship.

Judgmentalism is itself a manifestation of neurosis. People who thrive on condemning others may do so as an act of release. In truth—whether realized or not, even by them—they have a self-serving motive. Though loudly proclaiming an interest in rescuing sinners from the pit of hell, they actually may be expressing their own resentments. The indignation—however "righteous"—which is allowed to come out may be but that small portion of the iceberg above the surface. Beneath the waterline may lurk greater indignation which is far from righteous and which more than likely betrays their own sense of rejection.

If a congregation consistently enjoys hearing their pastor "lay it on the line," they themselves are in danger of hell-fire and damnation. They are possessed with hate. A Christian psychologist writes, "It is the frustrated, hostile persons who complain that the preacher does not preach about hell enough. They miss the vicarious enjoyment of hearing how bad the parishioners are and that they will go to hell if they do not respond."[1]

In the healthy fellowship there will be a conspicuous absence of judgmentalism. Even the very "elect" will tread softly through the first five verses of Matthew seven. Their own humility will preclude judgment of others.

In the healthy fellowship, living up to the Christian standard is encouraged through patient nurture, with the whole group playing some part. There is considerable exercise of tolerance. This is in contrast to the neurotic fellowship in which conformity is demanded overnight and discipline is by self-appointed rule, rather than by corporate consensus. But remember the healthy fellowship is not spineless or undisciplined, as noted in chapter five.

Hypocrisy vs Confessionalism

When impossible demands are placed upon us, and meeting them is the price of acceptance, we are placed in an intolerable circumstance. We are faced with the alternative of either forfeiting fellowship or resorting to hypocrisy. In the neurotic fellowship people are no more holy (often not so holy) as in the healthy fellowship. They just *appear* infallible. Everybody puts up the perfect front because no one dares to be the first to be honest. Woe unto the person who admits he doesn't measure up. In the church policed by a spiritual gestapo you have all the incentive needed for hypocrisy: fear of denunciation (public or private). No one is phony because he wants to be or admires it. He resorts to it because of expediency, the presumed lesser of two evils. It is an adjustment, however despicable, to the gap between what he is and what he thinks the group requires of him.

Hobart Mowrer, acclaimed for his emphasis on reality in therapy, writes, "One would think that the church would be the place where people could confront one another openly and honestly, since the church historically has made no pretense about man's condition and his need of redemption. But all too often the church is today a place where people hide behind Biblicism, and dogma, and theology."[2]

R. Lofton Hudson states, "It does seem unfortunate to me that religion has spent so much of its time trying to convince people what great sinners they are, only to turn around, as soon as they are 'on the program' and insist they demand of themselves that they be super! . . . If man asks us what to expect next, we are likely to dodge the whole issue or leave him with the impression that he has just inherited perfection, emancipation, and all lovelier-than-anybody traits."[3]

When the neurotic fellowship insists upon instantaneous flawlessness, it at once precludes any confession of sin or any feelers for additional help. Growth is stifled. How can you grow if you are expected to have already arrived at full stature?

Not only do those new in the faith bluff their way through, but sinners associated with the neurotic fellowship feel themselves to be among enemies, not among friends. Like the child who was spanked for breaking the window and thereafter reported no more offenses, sinners admit to nothing. Indeed they may never again darken the door of the church that has only reproach to offer.

In the healthy fellowship each person will be allowed the privilege of being human. His humanity will be no disgrace. It will be his honor on most occasions, and on those occasions when it seems to dishonor, he will be assured of understanding and forgiveness. Under those conditions there is no need for pretense. One can be honest and open about what he yet lacks, and reach for the tutelage of his spiritual peers (note: peers, not superiors or judges). In the healthy fellowship there will be a time and a place for the confession of anything from a noble vision to a heinous sin.

Because they can bring their humanity into the group, rather than checking it at the door like an ugly wrap, people will be free to "grow in grace," confronting their shortcomings before the entire fellowship or trusted members thereof. Because sinners witness the church in open repentance and frequent rededication, they will be reassured that they too will be accepted "though coming weak and vile." The healthy fellowship shares the same noble aspirations as those announced by the neurotic fellowship: the repentance of sinners and perfection of believers. Only the approach is different. That different approach was demonstrated by Jesus as he saved a very sinful woman from being stoned to death and then said, "Neither do I condemn thee; go and sin no more."

Rigidity vs Change

Because it is the nature of neurotics to be insecure when forced to cope with new circumstances, the neurotic fellowship will resist all change.

The neurotic fellowship will resist change in worship. Whether it be a Roman Catholic Church clinging to Mass in Latin or a small evangelical church holding fast to its formless form, the neurotic congregation will not feel that it has worshiped unless all is performed in the same old way. A certain man has entered the door of the church building only once in the past three years. A college drama group had been given charge of the Sunday morning worship service he attended. He declared the theatrics (which in all honesty were slightly overdone) were a manifestation of the devil's work.

The neurotic fellowship will be very slow to adopt new forms of mission. One reason evangelism is at a standstill in many churches is because their philosophy of evangelism is still that of John Wesley and the 1700s. Once, it worked, but not so well, if at all, anymore. Yet there is not the will or the know-how to change.

The neurotic fellowship usually is very reluctant to build, no matter how inadequate or ill-situated their facilities. The old building "where they prayed through" acquires a sacredness that borders on idolatry. One sizable congregation worshiped in a building that should have been demolished years before. Repeatedly they rejected efforts to start a building program. No matter what the proposal, the percentage of negative votes remained the same. People still entered the creaking doors every Sunday morning as though they were marching to Zion.

In the healthy fellowship there is no aversion to change, although change is always evaluated and must pass on its own merit. New approaches to worship are welcome for the freshness they bring. One of the greatest experiences our congregation has had in many years was the first time Gene Cotton presented a concert of sacred folk music during our morning worship service. Touched by Christ that morning were college students who had not responded to conventional "preaching services," no matter who preached.

In the healthy fellowship new forms of mission are explored. Personal evangelism is taken to like a duck takes to water. Members give themselves to forms of ministry that twenty years ago would have been considered irrelevant to the labors of Christ.

The healthy fellowship can move across town, if that is the Macedonia of the city. Or it can stay, even in a radically changing neighborhood and adopt a new style of community centered ministry. It can even replace certain church services with others which, though of different nature, do the job more effectively.

There remains yet one more comparison to be made between neurotic and healthy fellowships. We reserve that discussion to the following chapter.

---

[1]James R. Dolby, *I, Too, Am Man* (Waco, Texas: Word Books, 1969), p. 47.

[2]O. Hobart Mowrer, *The New Group Therapy* (Princeton: D. Van Nostrand Co., Inc. 1964), pp. 72-73.

[3]R. Lofton Hudson, *Helping Each Other Be Human* (Waco, Texas: Word Books, 1970), p. 12.

7

Uniformity Versus Individuality

Blessed is the church
which encourages individual growth,
for spiritual maturity shall mark her members.

Contemporary society places high premium on the dignity of man. Although this is a decidedly Christian concept, the neurotic fellowship finds it hard to accept. The church which stresses extreme uniformity denies the dignity of man by infringing upon his sovereignty. Modern man, well-educated, well-informed, affluent, and complex, resists any attempt to dictate to him. The church which insists on doing so will become increasingly burdensome to modern man, who eventually will go his lonely way.

Moreover, there is today a noticeable decline of the pastor's influence as a moral authority. Furthermore, what is true of the pastor's role is true of religion in general.

The church finds herself in the plight of a stern parent laying down the law to a rebellious teen-ager over whom he no longer has control. Downcast, he stands in the doorway calling after his errant child, "You can't. You can't." Only to see the object of his concern disappear down the road.

Because this new emphasis on human freedom has received its impetus from the world instead of from the church, much of that freedom is of a licentious, destructive nature. The enemy of man's soul has turned it to his advantage. The church cannot but lament the deplorable decay of today's society. The cry to be free has paved the way for sexual promiscuity, drunkenness, drug addiction and other forms of rampant ungodliness.

The church can and must speak out against these abuses. However, she must admit that at times her own intolerance has alienated her from those whom she might have saved. Many of these, had they been given their freedom in Christ, would never have resorted to the perverted freedom which now victimizes them.

Thus, the church must reclaim the doctrine of individual freedom. She must sanctify the dignity of man by bringing it under the canopy of righteousness. Paul shows us the way as he writes, "And be not conformed to this world: but be ye transformed by the renewing of your mind" (Rom. 12:2). Yes, I know the most autocratic of churches make that their theme. But they miss the point. They merely substitute models of conformity—themselves—for the world.

At best, this only improves conduct. It ignores the real concern of the text. Let the stress be on transforming the *mind*. Here is individuality without anarchy. Discipline has its place in the church. Christianity is mockery without it. However, discipline must come as the result of one's yielding himself to the Lordship of Jesus Christ, not an unwilling knuckling under to the dictates of a religious institution.

There is something especially blessed about hearing young people sing to the glory of God. I am always touched to see those who have been trained in the way in which they should go giving promise of walking therein. In our congregation one Sunday morning an event, which should have produced great joy within the congregation,

59

brought less than universal pleasure. Two of our fine young people blended their voices to sing a very traditional gospel song. They sang well, and with a depth of sincerity. However, his hair was longer than some would have liked it. Her skirt was shorter than some would have liked it.

The following Wednesday night in the midweek service, the president of our senior high youth fellowship rose to defend her peers. With ladylike graciousness and without a trace of rancor she said, "Just because some of us wear our hair a little long or our dresses a little short, you must not think we do not love the Lord just as much as you do. We may look a little funny to you, but if you could see into our hearts, you would know we are faithful to Christ and intend to stay that way." While this made no converts to modern styles, it did help us understand that difference is no occasion for suspicion.

Were we only to realize it, difference can be both stimulating and constructive. The church is at her dynamic best when freedom is not only permitted, but encouraged. Action and reaction provide the process by which growth occurs. We learn not from those who are like us, but from those who are unlike us. Thought is expanded when challenged by concepts foreign to existing patterns.

Uniformity can be stifling, both as it contributes to exclusivism and as it fosters monotony. R. Eugene Sterner cites a prime example. He writes, "Recently, I was a visitor in a class where the teacher was doing all the talking—and I do mean *all* of it! It was apparent that he was carefully saying all the accepted things in the accepted way, using all the right—and trite—words and phrases. The people, mostly older people—were nodding their heads in dutiful approval. He was droning on and they were drowsing through. There wasn't a single stimulating thought, not one bit of meaningful discussion, not a thing that was related to life as it is experienced today. That's the price of superficial agreement and shallow thought. Call it unity if you like. I don't call it that. There was no difference among them—there was only *indifference.*"[1]

I contrast the above class with a class which is perhaps the most popular one in our whole Sunday school. Every Sunday forty or more adults, most in their mid-fifties, share together in a brisk discussion period. There is a great variety of opinion within the group and all opinions are welcome.

One Sunday the teacher challenged the worthwhileness of one of the accepted ordinances of the church. No one drowsed through that session or nodded his head in dutiful agreement. Members of the class rose to the defense of the ordinance. They spoke with conviction which was infinitely more persuasive than any teacher's lecture. This suggests that the case for truth can only be effectively stated in an atmosphere of freedom and individual thought. Of course, this presumes a maturity among participants which means that differences of opinion can be expressed without jeopardy to fellowship.

The dynamic church will not be devoid of convictions. To the contrary, both theological beliefs and Christian standards will be firmly held. The strength of both will be that they are authentic. They will be authentic because each man will have forged his own. His faith and practice will have been tried by fire. There will be no robots reciting rote answers. Free to agree or disagree, all will have had to give a reason for the hope that is within them (1 Pet. 3:15).

The church should be that community in which a man can find himself. This applies whether one is a young person or simply one young in Christian faith. Each of us needs to discover those meanings in life which distinguish him as a moral and religious being. Until one knows what he believes, he cannot know who he is or have any sense of entity.

The church can commit one of two fundamental mistakes in attempting to help a man find himself. The first is to do all the finding for him—to leap out at him and say, "How could you be so confused when all the answers are right before you as plain as the nose on your face. Take our word for it and we'll see that you get on the right track." This compels him either to suppress all his questions or to tear loose from our grasp and flee further into the woods of confusion in order to protect his freedom.

These are both unenviable choices. It accounts for many of the belief-less believers who populate our churches, not to mention the unbelievers outside the church whose skepticism is but a reaction to the glib answers they heard when in church. In one sense a man cannot be *found;* he must *find*. *He finds only as he assimilates, and every man has to do that for himself.*

When the church pushes too hard for quick uniformity, the process of finding oneself is often aborted. If a person begins to think for himself, he seems to sense the disapproval of the church. The church becomes anxious about him and about his influence on the group. James Dolby writes of the squeeze in which the questing Christian finds himself, "The pressures from without may be fatal, they may destroy the possibility of self-discovery or personal honesty. They may press in till one gasps for air and pleads for mercy. I can hear the voices of the pressures from without—'Have you changed?' 'We don't understand you.' 'You had better be more careful.' 'Don't be naive.' 'How could you say that and be truly Christian?' 'He must be having difficulties in his spiritual life.' Often at this point people give up the task of self-discovery. These pressures are too great. We find ourselves inadequate to break through the walls of protection and provincialism. We have lost ourselves in all our complexity."[2]

The second mistake the church may make is to offer the lost no guidance at all, to stand back and say, "Just grope around for yourself. One way is as good as another." This leaves the seeker with no assurance of ever coming to an abiding belief. The expectation that one can become rooted and grounded in truth without ever being told what is truth is an absurdity. Freedom of thought is to be encouraged only if with it there is provided a sound biblical basis upon which convictions can be formed. Chaos will result otherwise. Witness the general lack of theological and ethical orientation among Protestants.

The church must speak with surety but without intimidation. Laying it on the line is helpful rather than detrimental *providing* the emphasis is on the word, not on the offender. Let the gospel, not the preacher be personal. In the relevant church it is not done as Jesus rebuking the devil in the wilderness, but as Jesus taking a little child and setting him in the midst of them. Laying it on the line can be an act of rejection or an act of redemption. The difference is in the focal point.

"So he is going into the ministry," I mused. Holding the letter in my hand, I recalled how fourteen years before this young man and his entire family had come into the congregation I then served. Many things must have attracted them, but I am sure that among them was my preaching. Fresh out of seminary, my sermons had little to commend them except their positive declarations from the Word of God. These were apparently the welcome sounds of certainty for which they had been searching.

---

[1]Article: "What Kind of Unity?" *Vital Christianity,* Vol. 90, No. 22 (November 1, 1970), p. 12.
[2]James R. Dolby, *I, Too, Am Man* (Waco, Texas: Word Books 1969), p. 5.

8

Shaping Creative Values

Blessed is the church
whose values are creative and positive,
for her people shall learn
the more excellent way.

As we have seen, even Christian people, because of impediments in their personalities, can be very miserable at times. There is yet another inner cause of unhappiness. This is not entirely unrelated to personality problems. In fact, it often is the result of them. I refer to a distorted value system.

One function of the church is to guide persons, individually and collectively, in the selection of goals which will bring to them the greatest measure of fulfillment in life. In the broadest sense, this is Christian education. Fulfilled people make a fulfilled church.

Several weeks ago my eight-year-old son and I were driving downtown. As we stopped at an intersection, immediately in front of us was a late model Cadillac, not just an ordinary Cadillac, but the big Fleetwood model. While we sat there waiting for the light to change, Marty said, "Wow! The lucky guy. I wish I were him."

"Who?" I asked, "the man in the Cadillac?"

"No," he replied, "the boy on the Honda beside him."

There is quite a spread of values among us. It has been said that one man's meat is another man's poison. We cannot understand another person's values until we have some insight into his felt needs. Jesus told a parable in which he referred to man's quest for the pearl of greatest value and, again, to a man's discovery of treasure buried in a field (Matt. 13:44-46). In each instance the man was willing to sacrifice all else in order to gain the pearl and the treasure. Each represented the supreme desire of his life.

The great range of values among us is explained by the fact that some of us expect to obtain fulfillment by one means and others by different means. With every one of us, however, our chosen means of fulfillment is to us the pearl of greatest price.

Our concept of fulfillment is influenced by at least three considerations:

1. Age. Values change with age because what might be fulfilling to a junior (i.e., a Honda) would not likely be fulfilling to a forty-year-old man (whose eye might be on the Cadillac). Felt needs and physical drives modify with age.

2. Our peer group. What appears to be fulfilling to our age group or social set suddenly looks good to us. If it brings them happiness it would do the same for us. Furthermore, if having that, doing that, or being that would enhance our standing with the group, we have an additional reason for being attracted.

3. Our assumed deficiencies. That area of life in which we feel most shortchanged is the area in which our values will tend to concentrate. For example, the girl who considers herself plain may disproportionately value beauty. We covet the pearl we do not have (while usually taking for granted all the pearls of which we are possessed). It's what we don't have—regardless of what we do have—that

makes us feel inferior. Any lack, keenly felt, makes us feel less than whole. It carries with it an element of stigma. Hence, we say of the great presumed equalizer, "If I had that, I would be happy" (fulfilled).

This happens not only to individuals, but also among whole segments of society. What was it that most disturbed the younger generation of twenty to thirty years ago? Poverty, with its attendant hardship and humiliation. So what are the treasured pearls of many persons now forty years of age and above? Affluence and status! So much so that these stereotype the establishment. What disturbs today's younger generation? A war which has lasted too long, and parental demands that youth fit into a mold indicative of status. And so what are the treasured pearls of today's youth? Peace and individuality. The two generations don't understand each other's values. Ironically, both only seek what they have felt most deprived of.

Our values are compensatory. We choose the pearls life has not passed out to us. Hence, they often are selected out of negative motivation. Is it any wonder, then, that we are not very objective about them?

If we do not feel adequately endowed, our value system will be greedy, self-centered, and, likely, destructive. Our incentive will be to lay hold on that which inflates our opinion of ourselves. If we do feel adequately endowed, our value system will be altruistic and constructive. Feeling no compulsion to compensate, we will be free to direct our attention outward rather than toward self.

We can live by positive values only if assured that "old No. 1" has been taken care of. The difference between selfish and unselfish people is simply that the latter feel equal and the former feel inferior.

The unhappy, unlikable, unsavory person is that because his values are negative. He is ruled by his feelings of inferiority, which in his search for equality compel him to act in destructive ways: selfishness, intemperance, instability, self-pity, hatefulness. Sin, be it expressed as sensualism or secularism, is but a misdirected attempt to find fulfillment. Sin is perversion of a normal desire, not infrequently perverted because feelings of inferiority push the desire to lustful proportions, an inordinate zeal causing the transgression of a moral law.

Our problem is that we make an erroneous assessment of what will fulfill us. Invariably, we choose values which minister only to surface needs, rather than to the underlying cause of our discontent.

Three of the biggest deceivers are materialism, popularity, and pleasure. All three seem to satisfy since each appeals strongly to self, and the self is all important to those suffering from feelings of inferiority. However, neither of the three can satisfy since they treat only the symptom and not the disease. Because they do treat the symptom, they actually bring a measure of brief relief, like aspirin. However, the pain soon returns, and we either must seek another dosage, or another medicine. Blessed are we if this time we turn to that which is therapeutic (as outlined in the following chapter) rather than that which only deadens the pain.

Remember, at least part of our value system is a reflection of our feelings of deprivation. The nature of the deprivation varies from person to person. Hence, when deceived about what is the pearl of greatest price, not all select the same false substitute. Those things which deceive us in purporting to be the means to fulfillment are not, of themselves, wrong. They are wrong only because our inferiority feelings lead us to place almost absolute value upon them, to view them as being in themselves adequate to bring us happiness. Let us look more closely at the philosophy behind our selection of the three most common deceivers mentioned above.

1. Materialism. Materialism means different things to different people. To those who lack a feeling of acceptance it may mean the way by which acceptance is achieved. The reasoning is, "After all, I've done well. They have to acknowledge my importance." This is so typical of the delusion of this age that money can buy almost anything, including acceptance. Or, again, still feeling rejected despite having done well, one may use materialism as a means to provide comfort in lieu of acceptance.

Of course, to those who feel insecure, materialism will stand for security. Whatever the felt need, materialism alone can't fill the bill. It can't buy acceptance. Comfort cannot suffice for relationships, and the person who is insecure isn't likely to be placated by any amount of savings.

2. Popularity. Popularity means just one thing to many of us: acceptance. The person who makes popularity his pearl of greatest price is so unsure of his desirability that he has to have mountainous evidence to confirm it. He craves more and more adulation.

He may want to be the star of the team. She may want to date every boy in school. Any symbol of popularity will be coveted. As we grow older, popularity contests become fewer. Often the only moral way a middle-aged person can demonstrate his popularity is to attempt foolishly to be the life of the party (the person who *is* the life of the party without trying probably is not seeking popularity. He simply is secure in his sense of acceptance and, therefore, is free to act like a clown).

Popularity, if depended upon exclusively, fails to satisfy. One can be popular without ever being close to anyone. The football star hears the roar of the crowd when he scores a touchdown, but who listens to him when he cries in the night over a broken romance? The detached person may have a lot of "friends," but he feels few, if any, would welcome his confiding in them.

3. Pleasure. Pleasure, when desired to bring us ultimate fulfillment, means just one thing: self-idolatry. Pleasure as the pearl of greatest price represents one's acknowledgment of either rejection or failure. Out of friends or out of luck, there is little to do but seek entertainment. The logic is, "Since I can't find pleasure in relationships or in achievement (or both), I will make it up to myself by having as good a time as I can."

Today's youth who turn to the drug scene have chosen exactly that approach to fulfillment. Drugs are looked upon as "instant pleasure," and, after all, we have instant everything else. Why not instant pleasure? If those youth who use drugs had the feeling of acceptance or of accomplishment, they would not need drugs.

Another reason for using drugs is the lack of opportunity to express oneself, as the result of domination, usually. Thus drugs serve the same purpose as liquor, a release from inhibition.

Pleasure, like the other two deceivers, cannot bring a lasting sense of fulfillment. We cannot live all our lives at the ball—and even if we could, who would want to?

When we seek satisfaction in wrong sources, we get wrong results. Not only do we miss fulfillment, but we often find our latter state worse than the beginning.

Jesus did not call the rich young ruler a sinner. He called him a fool. He was, of course, a sinner, but only because he had been fooled about what would fulfill him. He could have kept on tearing down barns and building bigger ones and never been satisfied. The reason is that he was treating the symptom rather than the disease. Jesus tried to treat the disease by getting the man to change his value system. "Go and sell that thou hast, and give to the poor," said Christ (Matt. 19:21). The point was to get the man to live for others instead of self, to exchange negative motivations for positive ones. The man rejected the advice and consequently "went away sorrowful."

Our moods indicate our success or failure in pursuit of fulfillment. Often, the chronically critical person is frustrated in his search for fulfillment, and is out to punish others for it. Likewise, the despairing person has not found fulfillment, and is on the verge of giving up all hope of doing so.

We do not give up easily in our quest for happiness. Most of us doggedly continue the process of buying and selling to get the pearl of greatest price and digging to unearth the hidden treasure. For us, fulfillment is just around the corner. We haven't achieved it yet, but the promise seems to be there. Again and again, however, when we think we've found it, we discover we have been deceived. Like the old prospector, there seems little for us to do but keep on looking.

The reason we have in our churches some of the dour people we do is because disillusionment has set in. This is especially true among the middle-aged. Many have never had it so good materially as they do now. Yet their nice homes and nice cars are hollow shells. These same people have few meaningful relationships with friends. Perhaps they never did enjoy great popularity, or, if they did, dwindling contact has now largely isolated them. Disillusioned people are dull people. They are sullen, cynical, and sedentary. If their spirit is the dominating spirit of the congregation, it is not a mature church.

The mature church will be one in which positive, creative values are always exalted. Deceptive values will be exposed and "a more excellent way" will be presented. That more excellent way is the subject of our next chapter.

9

What Makes Us Happy?

*Blessed is the church
where discipline is Christ-centered,
for her witness shall be genuine.*

A young college student, just after his thrilling conversion, cried out in a sudden burst of compassion for those still in the dilemma from which he had just been delivered, "Young people are looking for happiness, but they can't find it!" Why is it that today's younger generation, plus much of the older generation as well, cannot find happiness? Because they are committed to the wrong value system.

Before some of us can ever find fulfillment we shall have to drastically change our thinking about what is the pearl of greatest price. The Apostle Paul experienced a revolution in his value system. This is his testimony, "I count all things but loss for the excellency of the knowledge of Christ Jesus my Lord: for whom I have suffered the loss of all things, and do count them as dung, that I may win Christ" (Phil. 3:8). Number one values for Paul fell all the way to the level of waste, whereas Christ came to become the ultimate—even absolute—value in his life.

The beginning of all fulfillment (happiness) is to make Christ your pearl of greatest price, your number one desire.

"BE-ATTITUDES" FOR THE CHURCH

There are three things in life which every one of us must experience in order to be fulfilled. We crave these whether afflicted with feelings of inferiority or not, but to gain them is to overcome all sense of inadequacy and worthlessness. Now here is the important part: These three can best be realized, not in direct pursuit, but as the by-product of a redemptive, creative relationship with Jesus Christ.

1. We want acceptance. That is, we want to be esteemed by others, to be taken seriously as persons, to have a place in the lives of others. Acceptance presumes a commitment from others; popularity does not. No one believes in himself until he is irrevocably convinced that others believe in him. Feelings of inferiority are rooted in the suspicion that the world (at least that portion of the world important to us) considers us second-rate by at least one of its standards of measurement.

Remember: our values are frequently compensatory, we aspire to that which we feel has been deprived us. Hence, if a person feels rejected, what will be his big ambition in life? To find acceptance, to win esteem and praise. A number of years ago a very attractive young woman set her sights on Hollywood. Her ultrareligious and authoritarian parents were nearly impossible to please. Apparently feeling rejected, she decided an actress's acclaim was what she wanted.

Grossly misled, she sold herself into white slavery to gain that prize. Tragically, her path did not lead to the silver screen but to a life of cheap harlotry. Deprived of acceptance by her parents and even the popularity of movie fans, she had to settle for the illicit love of a small time gangster by whom she bore a child who grew up to be a murderer.

We want acceptance. God wills that we have it. However, we find it not by placing it first on life's agenda, but by turning our affections, full force, toward Christ.

72

When we do this, Christ brings us acceptance in two glorious ways.

First, he personally accepts us. His cordial invitation extends to all, "Come unto me . . ." (Matt. 11:28). There is no greater feeling of acceptance than the experience of salvation. In Christ's great forgiveness of our sins we are overwhelmed by his grace, and revel to be embraced—vile though we may have been—by the eternal, omnipotent God, the most important being in all the universe. Imagine such standing!

We are accepted the way the prodigal son was as he stood there on the doorstep of home, enveloped by the arms of a forgiving father who declared to the rest of the family and to the household servants, "This [is] my son." What rank for one fresh from the pigpen!

We are accepted the way Mary Magdalene was as she knelt at the feet of Jesus, washing his feet with her tears, wiping them with her flowing hair, and anointing them with perfume.

Oh, the exhilaration of knowing, "Jesus loves me! Jesus loves even me! Heaven accepts me." With an endorsement like that, one can accept himself. E. Stanley Jones writes, "Inferiority complexes, which are at the back of so much mere half-living are cured more radically by conversion than by anything else."[1]

Unfortunately, many of us do not take seriously the flattery of Christ's forgiveness of sin. We do not take at face value the equation between the cross and what we are worth in God's sight. We are not overwhelmed by his grace, as theory discloses we should be. Now this is the tragedy of that: Consequently we do not experience full conversion, that is, we are not totally delivered from our hang-ups. Although our salvation is assured, we are not freed of our troublesome attitudes, and still need another touch.

73

Secondly, Christ makes us acceptable. Although he can take us as we are, not many others can. Therefore, he provides a "new birth." No matter what we have been, we can begin again, transformed into new creatures. There is no therapy for the human personality like spiritual regeneration. Nothing else can so drastically make the cantankerous compatible, the perverse pure, the fretful fearless, the proud humble, and the unreasonable reasonable. No longer need we *feel* unworthy because no longer need we *be* unworthy.

A woman said of her husband who recently had been converted, "Two weeks ago I would've loved to have gotten rid of him. Now I wouldn't take a million dollars for him." That's acceptance!

Because of its strategic role in affording us a feeling of acceptance, the authentic church will place heavy emphasis upon a personal conversion experience.

2. We want achievement, to feel that we have ability, that we are needed, that we contribute. For one person that desire may be satisfied with something as unpretentious as being a good pie-maker whose baking delights her family and friends. At the opposite extreme it may be something as outstanding as landing on the moon.

No one feels fulfilled until he can say, "I have been here and I have left my mark. It may not be a great work, but it is significant, and it is distinctively mine." If one does not feel that sense of achievement, he suffers condemnation. It seems to him that his life is worthless, and that, hence, as a person, he is worthless.

The Ambitious Guest in Hawthorne's story by that title pushes back his chair from a hearty supper of bear meat and addresses himself to his hosts. His cheeks glow and his eyes flash as he begins to tell of a fire burning in his soul. "As yet," he says, "I have done nothing. Were I to vanish from the earth tomorrow . . . not a soul would ask, 'Who was he? . . .' But I cannot die till I have achieved my destiny. Then, let Death come. I shall have built my monument!" Thus did the Ambitious Guest express for each of us the desire to achieve and to contribute.

We want achievement. It is part of God's plan. God said to Adam, "Be fruitful" (Gen. 1:28). However, when we place achievement first in our lives, being greedy for success, it becomes forbidden fruit. It leads to death. If, on the other hand, we seek Christ first, he, in turn, leads us to achievement. When we set out to glorify ourselves, even if we reach the top rung of the ladder, we can only look out over our conquests and say in disillusionment, "Is that all there is?" Again, if we seek first to glorify Christ, we can say with great contentment, "My meat is to do the will of him who sent me."

Christ extends the greatest invitation to achievement when he beckons, "Follow me, and I will make you fishers of men." If we want to contribute something that is lasting and of value, we should enlist in his cause, that of healing broken humanity through divine love.

Dr. Paul Carlson, a Christian physician and medical missionary, gave his life during the Congolese uprising in 1964. He was there in the Congo by his own choice, because he found fulfillment in ministering to the jungle natives. He had visited there briefly in 1961, during which time he wrote home, "It does something to you to work out here." Not long thereafter, he volunteered to return. Why? Because Dr. Paul Carlson found a sense of achievement as a missionary he never found in private practice.

In his early years, George W. Truett assumed the pastorate of a struggling Texas congregation. "I'll give my life . . . the best and all of it if need be," he said, "to make this into the greatest church in America." Forty years later when George Truett retired, he left behind the largest Baptist church in this country. That's achievement!

75

Is there any greater sense of achievement—no matter how meager the task—than when Christ says at the close of the day, "Well done, thou good and faithful servant?" Man knows no greater dignity than to be a partner with God, a worker together with the saints of all ages, than to be able to say, I'm helping to make a better world.

Because a sense of achievement is so vital to individual fulfillment, the happy church will lay heavy stress on the importance of deep, personal commitment to the mission of Jesus Christ.

3. We want autonomy, to be free to determine our own course and to express ourselves in our own creative way.

To have a sense of identity we must establish and protect our powers of self-government. Even as God instructed Adam to be fruitful, he also said, "and have dominion" (Gen. 1:28). A patient recovering from surgery once said to me, "After while you get to feeling like you are not a person." This is a rather common phenomenon in hospitals, although seldom articulated so profoundly.

Put to bed dressed in the nondescript hospital attire, told when to go to sleep and when to wake up, given shots or pills at the discretion of the staff, told what are their confines, physically examined at a moment's notice, and too sedated or ill to have a will of their own, patients do indeed lose their sense of personhood. Their autonomy has been taken away.

The point is that something very similiar happens when we yield ourselves the servants of sin. Nothing more degrades a man than to be ruled by a passion or habit over which he has no control. I have seen patients in state mental hospitals beg like puppies for their ten o'clock cigarette. I heard an old man tell at an AA meeting how, as an alcoholic in his younger days in order to buy booze, he would sell his summer clothes in the winter and his winter clothes in the summer.

We want to be free. Yet when we place our desire to be free as the number one value in life, we then become slaves. The secret is to reverse that process. As we place Christ the number one value in life—become his slave— then we are made free. We must accept what he says about sin, about its power of enslavement, about what he says *is* sin. On the positive side, we must be ruled by a compelling desire to please him, to imitate his sinlessness, to seek those pleasures that are devotional rather than sensual.

There is no greater form of self-expression than a life that is free in Christ to praise and serve God. There is no greater level of liberty than that of being free in Christ to say no to what one will and yes to what one will. There is no greater awareness of identity than being able to say, Under God I rule my course.

John Newton was a lustful, heartless slave trader who deliberately set out to disregard all moral restraint. His own confession was, "I went to Africa that I might be free to sin to my heart's content." However, on board ship returning to England, he repented in deepest agony for his licentiousness. The change of masters brought a different confession, framed in his immortal hymn,

> "Amazing grace! how sweet the sound,
>   That saved a wretch like me!
> I once was lost, but now am found,
>   Was blind, but now I see."

Because there is no fulfillment short of the creative expression of our individual genius, the dynamic church will exalt the Lordship of Jesus Christ, by which divine will becomes the salvation of our own will.

---

[1]E. Stanley Jones, *Is the Kingdom of God Realism?* (New York: Abingdon Press, 1955), p. 191.

10

Understanding the Generation Gap

*Blessed is the church
where all age groups are appreciated,
for it shall be known as God's happy family.*

We've heard much talk the past several years about the "generation gap." This is no figment of the imagination. It is a real chasm. But it is not new. Nor is it limited to just two generations. There is a gap between *each* generation, across the human life-span.

Every generation has its own vested interests. Out of this inevitably comes discord between age groups. Our needs, desires, philosophies, values, tastes, and even many of our hang-ups often are related to where we stand along the continuum of life. More than is commonly realized, the kind of person each of us is can be attributed to age factors.

We cannot close the generation gap. There is reason to doubt the wisdom of doing so even if we could. Somewhat mysteriously we detect the handiwork of God here. Each generation has its own special contribution to make. For the good of the whole of man, generation distinctives should survive. More than that, however, generations must learn to live together harmoniously, without insisting upon conformity from one another.

Though the generation gap cannot be closed, bridges can and should be built. This is best done by promoting understanding between generations. If one generation comes to know why it thinks and behaves as it does, this is a beginning. If that generation comes, furthermore, to know why other generations think and act quite differently, considerable concord will result.

Generation gaps have great ramifications within the church. Here generations share in worship, service, fellowship, and witness. Approaches to each of these vary greatly from the young to the old. The varying degrees of emphasis on each of these is even more pronounced. It is difficult to arrive at a common theology among the generations. Uniform standards are an impossibility. Here, then, is a potential source of conflict, not unlike that which goes on in many households.

Recently, a troubled pastor, confronted by growing animosity between generations within his congregation, asked, "How can I please both sides?" Whether the church is healthy or unhealthy depends to a large extent upon how well the generation gap is bridged.

Let us consider some age groups within the average congregation, with special emphasis on their respective characteristics and needs. (This is not to imply that every member of any given generation complies totally to a certain stereotype, but, generally speaking, similarities among persons of the same generation afford a valuable guide when working with groups of people.)

Youth

The healthy church will be aware of the needs of youth carefully ascertaining those needs and gearing to meet them. Even more important, however, than programming is the attitude of the rest of the congregation toward the youth of the church. Adults should guard against adopting either a judgmental or a condescending approach to young people. Youth find both equally offensive.

The church's ministry to youth must recognize the basic struggles of youth. What was said in chapter nine is especially applicable to youth.

1. The struggle for recognition. Youth are attempting to "crash" the adult world. As with any minority group they are looking for equality, the equality which, of necessity, has been denied them during the years of childhood. Equality is conditioned upon mutual respect. Thus every youth wants to be heard. He does not feel heard when "put down" or ignored. He looks upon the adult community and says, "I would like to join 'em." He then goes forth to make his first timid overtures.

If these overtures are warmly received—even when they cannot always be agreed with—he moves forward with more confidence and increasing productivity. He reasons, "The church is fair and open-minded. There is a place for me here. I am accepted as a person."

On the other hand, if a youth's first overtures are spurned, he may speak more vociferously and become increasingly reactionary. If repeatedly denied equality, he likely will withdraw from the fellowship—in some cases, for life.

The healthy church will place youth in leadership positions and utilize youth in the church's worship and service. Most importantly, whenever youth and adults intermingle, whether in formal or informal settings, adults will be good listeners.

2. The struggle for independence. Erickson describes adolescence as the period of search for identity. Every youth strives to be an entity in his own right. He feels he must break away from parental and social domination. Subjection thwarts him in his attempt to stamp himself as an individual. Hence, the church is most offensive to

youth at the point of insistence upon conformity to standards. These may be resisted not only because they are "too strict," but because they represent the thinking of the older generation and, hence, represent a threat to youth's own identity.

Much of the motivation behind extreme dress and grooming is an aggravated attempt to preserve youth's sense of self. Allowed more individuality within the church, youth would not have to go outside the church for acceptance as individuals. In the relevant church young people are allowed to present their youthfulness proudly. They are encouraged to express their tastes and viewpoints. There is an absence of defensiveness between the generations, because generation distinctives are welcome.

3. The struggle for new experiences. Toy cars and dolls no longer suffice. Youth are looking for bold new thrills. Puberty and wider exposure to the world have vastly multiplied emotional appetites. Physical and intellectual capacities have likewise burgeoned. Youth want to experience more and do more than is sometimes advisable. Here the church often appears as a great stumbling block. At the very time when youth feel driven to experiment, the church seems always to be saying, No! No!

The church in its ministry to youth makes a fatal mistake if it chooses to emphasize the "thou shalt not" approach. Without denying youth's independence and urge to adventure, the church must find a way to save youth from indiscriminate experimentation with sex, drugs, alcohol, and other forms of vice. To avoid conflict with youthful drives, the church must give early attention to education, focusing first on moral principles and values long before express habits and pleasures become a battleground between the generations. Here the church must work closely with the home to instill love for virtue and decency, which build restraint.

4. The struggle for meaning. Youth are searching for "something to believe in." This is where the church should shine, and will shine, provided certain considerations are kept in mind.

If the church's message of Christian faith is to be espoused by youth, that message must be presented with intellectual integrity. I sometimes have blushed over answers given to bright young students by parents, Sunday school teachers, and even pastors. Replies or pronouncements which are glib, simplistic, and downright nonsensical only diminish youth's admiration for the church. Youth can accept the fact that faith transcends reason, but they will not listen to naive explanations which insult their mental capacity. If the church is to speak with authority, her answers must be on the same scholastic level as those of secular education.

If the church's message of faith is to be espoused by youth, it must be relevant to their questions, their fears, their temptations, their concerns. We identify only with that which touches our lives. Youth are attracted to that church which leads them to experience God as a real and loving Presence, which gives authentic reasons for choosing good over evil, which channels their altruistic ambitions into meaningful service, which affords genuine hope, and which dignifies the existence of man.

It is a vital church whose young people thank God that an honest attempt is made to understand them and to meet their needs.

Young Adults

How well the needs of young adults are met may well determine their relationship with the church for the rest of their lives. Many young people are lost to the church at the time of marriage. In numerous cases this has been a long-contemplated break, awaiting only departure from home. In other cases, however, it represents a failure on the part of the church to serve young families.

1. A time of freedom. Young married adults usually are just beginning to experience being "on their own." They are free to sleep in on Sunday morning or to take a weekend holiday. No longer can the church rely on mom and dad to get them to service. The church has to be more solicitious and more enticing. An additional and unwelcome form of freedom comes in that old associations are broken or at least altered. Wedding bells do have a way of breaking up "that old gang of mine."

The just-married couple may need to find new points of relatedness to the church family. Old allegiances are broken, but new ones have not been formed. To counteract this disconjunctiveness the church will need to create a feeling of togetherness among young adults and to act quickly to incorporate newlyweds and newcomers into this group. Fellowship activities are a must. Service projects and a missionary circle for young women are most helpful. The young adult Sunday school teacher is a crucial factor also. He (or she) needs to be a catalyst around which the whole group gathers. Together with his or her spouse, the two of them serve as heads of the "family," preserving something of the security of that nest so recently left.

2. A time of adjustment. The young couple face the monumental task of adjusting to one another and to their new roles as husband and wife. Later, they must adjust to children and to their roles as parents. Many a crisis can arise during these periods of adjustment. Hopefully, the pastor will have married the couple and will have excellent rapport with them. If he did perform their ceremony, he will have counseled with them and led them in a discovery of potential problem areas. If and when difficulties

arise, the couple should feel free to discuss them with him. Of course, the church also will need to be close at hand in the event of illness or tragedy.

3. A time of heavy responsibility. The young couple, if starting "from scratch," face a long, uphill struggle in becoming established financially. Income is usually stretched to the limit. The husband may work long hours, or study evenings, in order to gain a promotion. The wife may work. The young couple will find it very easy to say they "don't have time" for the church. First things may not come first with young couples who are faced with the problem of rethinking values and establishing priorities. The young couple also may be defensive about their stewardship obligations. Feeling the press of financial obligations, they may resent the church asking for its portion, or feel guilty about "not being able" to give their fair share.

Still, the young couple have a wealth of ability which the church must appropriate, both for the execution of its program and the preservation of the couple's souls. The church will need to be discriminatory in what it asks of young adults, being careful not to ask too much or too little and to ask the right things.

Congregations which make good use of their young adults are typically zealous, progressive, and efficiently managed. However, congregations made up predominantly of young families frequently run into trouble. Because of their immaturity and the tendency to become too intimate, young adults find that misunderstandings can easily occur and fracture beautiful friendships. This is especially true if the pastor and his wife are young adults and allow themselves to be drawn into a clique.

Forward-looking is the church that conserves its young adults and guides them into patterns of living that will bless them and the church in years to come.

Middle Age

In most congregations it can be said, "As the middle-aged go, so goes the church." This is true for two reasons. (a) The middle-aged usually constitute the largest single age group within the church. (b) The church usually depends to a very large extent upon the middle-aged for its leadership and its financial support. To a greater extent than can be said of other age groups, the characteristics of middle age are both assets and liabilities to the church. Middle age is typically a time of conservation.

1. The middle-aged person wants to conserve his investments. He has spent his youth getting what he has. Usually, he'll settle for that. His loss of incentive explains this. He probably has enough to be comfortable. There is less urgency. He probably recognizes the inevitable: not all his dreams are going to be realized. There is less hope. He almost certainly has less physical ambition. Even if the spirit is willing, the flesh sometimes is weak.

2. The middle-aged person wants to conserve his identity. The middle-aged person is not inclined toward flexibility. Being identified with the world the way it is (the world with which he grew up and which he helped to shape), he will not welcome change. Change makes him feel like an outsider, a stranger. Destroy the status quo and you destroy him, because he has invested himself in it. He *is* the status quo. Change forces adjustment. Adjustment is normal for the youth, abnormal for the middle-ager. That's why middle age has been called the period when the broad mind and the narrow waist trade places.

3. The middle-aged person wants to conserve time. He often is a "bug" on the news, listening to it two, three, four times a day, perhaps unable to retire until after the eleven o'clock edition. At the same time he may abandon all interest in scholarship. His great interest in the news is

85

attributable to two things: First, he is concerned with how fast the world (his world) is eroding, to what extent his values are being threatened. Second, in the temporality of events he is painfully reminded of his own temporality.

The middle-aged person (more probably the man) often has an obsession with the present. This is because he is so conscious of being a creature of time. With the passing of youth and the press of age, his mortality suddenly strikes him. Those of middle age who are well adjusted will not spend their time worrying about growing old. They will avail themselves of such opportunities for pleasure and relaxation as their success will provide.

What does this period of conservation mean to the church? On the positive side it means the backbone of the church will come from this age group. For good reason most enterprises and institutions depend heavily on the middle-agers. Ordinarily, they are qualified, loyal, dependable, and hard working. Often they are unselfish to a fault and allow themselves to be used. They require a minimum of care from those who rely on them. If life is fulfilling to them, they are congenial and cooperative.

On the negative side, because of their conservatism, those of middle age may impede the progress of the church. In their suspicion of change they are apt to discard many good ideas. When young ministers leave the church and rail out against its rigidity, usually it is this segment of the church to which their ire is directed. The middle-agers quite naturally feel the church should be managed as they manage their own lives. Don't risk much indebtedness, don't be too visionary in your goals and don't encourage a shift in values. On the other hand, many middle-aged people do not feel this way, and these stand at the forefront of all constructive programs of the church.

The ministry of the church to the middle-agers will be to keep them contemporary in their thinking and involved in the world around them. It will be to remind them of their immortality and to reassure them that whatever their disappointments (which has been called a middle-aged disease), they should not underestimate their achievements and should judge success by other than secular values. If the church can save its middle-agers from despair, negativism, and boredom, it will serve them well.

The church which is extremist and always championing change for the sake of change disrupts the serenity of its middle-aged constituents and robs them of the stability they crave. On the other hand, the narrow, reactionary church also will do these persons great harm by entrenching their alienation from a changing world.

The church and the middle-ager greatly need each other. Each is profoundly affected by the other. Strong is the church where the influence is mutually wholesome.

Old Age

The age of the elderly has been termed a period of simplification. Life is less complex for those living in the sunset of life. Many struggles are now past. One needs less money, fewer activities, not quite so many friends. He doesn't have so many unanswered questions, unresolved conflicts, or burning ambitions. In old age we don't need so much, but what we do need we need very much. The church figures largely in seeing to it that these needs are met.

1. A sense of serenity. If a man's beliefs have been authentic through his earlier years, they will be of inestimable value in his old age. Knowing what he believes will buttress him against the threats of illness, loneliness, and death. His "attitudinal values" (Frankl's term) will be his most supportive resource.

The church will need to reinforce the faith of the elderly. It certainly should not debunk it. This strikes at the one security the elderly possess. I remember a seventy-year-old man who had just been told he had an inoperable malignancy. Day after day as I visited him in the hospital he shared his beliefs. It was really a form of preaching—and very good preaching at that. Supposedly, I was the audience of one. Yet, I was not the target of his affirmations of faith. *He* was. One day, in a moment of candor, he said, "You see, Brother Huttenlocker, I'm trying to convince myself of these things."

This was no indictment of his faith, for his tactic was a wise one. For many years he had believed the things he had been repeating to me each day now. He wanted only to confirm in his own mind the correctness of those beliefs. Each day as he preached I had helped him do this by listening, interrupting only briefly to reassure him that what he was saying was indeed a trustworthy tenet.

2. A sense of significance. Remember, our sense of personhood derives from three experiences: (a) acceptance, (b) achievement, and (c) autonomy. From the moment of retirement, the elderly person is prone to suffer loss of the sense of achievement, particularly if his occupation was a substantial part of his self-expression. As he becomes more infirm, inevitably he also begins to lose some of his autonomy. The children begin to make some of their parents' decisions (which almost always provokes strong protest). It seems as though individuality is being taken away. Is there any help for such persons?

The church can help. First, the pastor can intercede by interpreting to the elderly the rationale behind the solicitous intervention into their affairs. Second, the church can contribute substantially to the elderly person's sense of achievement by emphasizing his role in the church. The church will provide him with opportunities to be productive (even when he is no longer able to teach a class or serve on a board). The elderly make great pray-ers.

They have the faith and they have the time. They can be assigned ministries of cheer: making phone calls to shut-ins, sending get well cards, doing certain forms of record-keeping, and making other significant contributions.

One reason many elderly people become self-pitying and complain about how "the church is not what it used to be" is that they feel the church has put them on the shelf. It is no longer "my church." It is "their church." One of the choicest fellowships my wife and I have ever enjoyed with any Sunday school class was with the class of elderly persons in a former pastorate. Every month we were guests at their Thursday night potluck. We reveled in their cheery, positive outlook on life. We encouraged them in their numerous projects.

When I was out of town on preaching assignments, my wife took our boys and went just the same. I could always depend on the class having "a good season of prayer" for their pastor while he was away. They felt significant, and they were! We cherished their contribution.

3. A sense of need. While they do not like to be reminded of it or have it overly compensated for, the elderly feel a troublesome dependency on others. Even when the help needed is minimal, the threat is there of complete helplessness. The church can be quietly available, providing it unpretentiously so the recipient is not robbed of his dignity. The feeling, "I have a lot of friends among the church people, and they will not let me down," means a great deal to the elderly and is best supported by appropriate and timely deeds.

The church can be "one big, happy family" with all generations serving and being served. Whether this noble ambition is realized or not depends upon the programming of the congregation, coupled with wholesome respect for the differing values and needs of respective generations.

11

Happiness Is a Happening

Blessed is the church
whose worship celebrates the living God,
for it shall be vital and strong and effective.

Lance Webb told about a little boy who, while being shown around the church by its pastor, spotted a bronze plaque on one wall of the narthex. With childlike curiosity he inquired about its meaning. "Well," answered the pastor, "those are the names of men who died in the service."

The boy responded by asking, "In which service, the nine o'clock or the eleven o'clock?"

Just how many casualties are there during the average Sunday worship service? Have they ever been counted? Occasionally an honest soul will complain, "It just kills me to go to church." Perhaps there should be a plaque in every narthex honoring those courageous souls who die a thousand deaths in order to be able to say they have been to church.

What makes the difference between a service that is a joy to attend and one that is torture to endure? Certainly not all worship experiences are tedious. Who of us has not been to church and come away revived, exclaiming, "This has been like heaven," or words expressing a similar thought? Obviously, given the proper components, worship can be the re-creative experience God intends it to be.

In the second chapter of Mark we read about a most unusual church service. Few of the traditional elements of worship were present. There was no choir anthem, no liturgy, probably no pastoral prayer and—most unusual of all—no offering. Even the place was different, since the congregation did not meet in an elaborate church building, but in a humble home in Capernaum. Yet, this service had such great appeal that there was an overflow crowd with not so much as even standing room. Worship leaders would do well to copy the success formula of that service.

First of all, the Word was preached. Now, in the most modern services it is not unusual for the scriptures to be *seen* on the communion table and *read* during the order of worship. But is the Bible *preached* from the pulpit?

See Jesus as he rises to address the congregation. His only vestments are a penetrating gaze and a commanding eloquence. Either reading from a scroll (such as was delivered to him that day in the synagogue) or quoting from memory, Jesus "preached the word unto them" (Mark 2:2). The Word of Life came to life through his exposition. We don't know his text, but we can be sure the sermon was comparable to that never-to-be-forgotten one on the mount.

It is sad that the romance of preaching seems lacking among so many pastors today. After I had spoken to a group of seminary students, one of them came up to me with a grin and said, "It kind of puts the excitement back into preaching."

There is good reason to believe that sound preaching still can attract and influence people widely. Doberstein (Thielicke's translator) writes, "What I and many of my colleagues hear . . . is that people want good preaching. Again and again, highly intellectual lay people, who love the church and the Lord of the church, say to us, 'Why

91

can't we have better preaching?' "[1] Doberstein continues, "Wherever we find, even in this day, a vital, living congregation we find at its center vital preaching."[2] Elton Trueblood adds, "There have been no changes in our culture which alter the fact that the spoken word may be a powerful force in human life."[3]

Before preaching can ever reclaim its rightful inheritance, preachers will need to accept two biblical affirmations: (1) that it pleases God "by the foolishness of preaching to save them that believe" (1 Cor. 1:21), and (2) that the gospel "is the power of God unto salvation to everyone that believeth" (Rom. 1:16). Like twin pillars, neither of these Pauline professions can be removed or even weakened without causing the roof to topple in upon the blind man who desecrates them.

Dr. Wallace Fisher states the preacher's position so perfectly:

"Called to be a colaborer with Christ, he places his confidence in the gospel of God and the human activity of preaching. Lack of confidence in either maims the church's exercise of Christ's ministry. . . . Let any ordained minister of Christ's church come before the tribunal of biblical evidence to get his bearings if he does not believe that God was in Christ, that scriptures witness to that mighty deed, and that preaching is a primary means for communicating this news to man."[4]

Preaching is as much God's way as is the cross God's way. Preaching and the gospel go together like love and marriage. Preaching apart from the Bible reduces the preacher's effort to human striving and his message to earthly knowledge. Conversely, without the preacher, the Bible is a priceless coin lost in an "ecclesiastical ghetto."

If the gospel cannot quicken, then God has left the preacher in an untenable position. What recourse has he but to say, "I will not make mention of him, nor speak any more his name" (Jer. 20:7-10). Merrill Abbey reminds us, "Any adequate theology of preaching builds on the conviction that God not only commissions and sends preachers; he is himself present in true preaching."[5] P. T. Forsyth went so far as to intimate that there is a "sacramental quality" to a sermon.[6]

The Apostle Paul cried out, "Woe to me if I preach not the gospel!" Had there been no gospel there would have been no mandate to preach. The preacher's task is not to entertain, but to proclaim the Good News. How unthinkable for him to draw his major thought from the dust of classical literature or the ashes of current events when he has access to the rich soil of God's word.

In the dynamic church there is no weariness with the *ad nauseam* of the pulpit, no drowsy members, no excessive absenteeism, no legitimate ridicule of the preaching. Instead, those who hunger and thirst after righteousness rise up and call blessed the pastor who helps to fill them.

The second attraction of this service in Capernaum was the preeminence of Christ. He *was* the service. Without him there would have been nothing. Everyone's attention was focused on him. The crowd had gathered as the result of the news "that he was in the house."

The most uplifting worship services are those in which Jesus Christ is praised. Nothing enables sitting together in heavenly places like the name of Jesus. Nothing bids the timid heart to speak like the presence of Jesus. When Christ presides over a service it takes on the celebration of a wedding feast. People still come to church with the age-old request, "We would see Jesus" (John 12:21).

The living church will speak often of Jesus, while avoiding pretentious mention of God just for effect. Project the image of a dour, distant—aloof—Deity upon a congregation and suddenly hearts are frozen. Worship that has dignity as its primary objective serves nothing except the leader's ascetic taste. In the vital church there is freedom of the spirit. The congregation is not inhibited, but encouraged to "come boldly to the throne of grace."

The service was over, but he refused to leave. The determined little fellow of six or seven became quite demonstrative when his mother by sheer force attempted to dislodge him from the pew. "I came here to see God," he wailed, "and I'm not leaving 'til I do." Maybe his expectations were a little too ambitious—and he might have been just a little "spoiled"—but still he had a point. After all, it is that encounter with the Divine which attracts worshipers to the Lord's house.

Yet, do we know what we ask? Consider Isaiah's classic experience in which he "saw the Lord sitting upon a throne, high and lifted up" (Isa. 6:1). Many hold this to be a model worship experience. But suppose we could reproduce it every Sunday morning at nine or eleven o'clock. Would we fill our churches? Not likely. Rather, we probably would empty them. Ah, but if we could duplicate that experience in the little home in Capernaum, we would have overflow crowds every Sunday. The truth is, when we worship, we are not seeking trauma. We are seeking tenderness. This we find best expressed in the lowly Nazarene.

God is most personable in the person of Jesus Christ. God's charms are the gentle smile and pleasant voice of the man of Galilee. "High and lifted up" is not for most of us. We respond best to the Lord when we find him "meek and lowly of heart." The most universal symbol of acceptance in all the world is the figure of Jesus standing with arms outstretched saying, "Come unto me, all ye that labor and are heavy laden" (Matt. 11:28).

The joyous congregation may often be heard singing:

Blessed assurance, Jesus is mine!

O what a foretaste of glory divine!

Heir of salvation, purchase of God,

Born of his Spirit, washed in his blood.

Even avowed sinners feel welcome in the presence of Jesus. The church that wishes to attract rather than repel the unconverted will exalt Christ. Many will find the "light of his glory and grace" irresistible. A woman of the streets burst in upon Christ while he dined with a rich man. A crooked tax collector invited Jesus to go home with him. A dying thief begged him for pardon.

Jesus is Lord of the people. He is God with dust on his feet. Because he is one of us, he wins us. God is love, but the warmth and understanding of Christ do most to convince us of it.

This service in Capernaum had a third appeal, equally essential as the first two. There was action! God's power was asserted. There was a demonstration of his mighty works.

Having great faith in the healing ministry of Christ, several men brought a friend, one afflicted with palsy. Finding no way to get through the crowd which thronged the house, the men ingeniously invented a way. They climbed up on the roof, removed several tiles and lowered their friend on a stretcher right into the Lord's presence. Jesus was greatly impressed with their tremendous display of faith and responded by instantly healing the man.

Most people who "die" in church do so out of boredom. They become fatalities not because the building is too hot or too cold, not because the seats are too hard and not because the pastor's message is too bold. They are just simply bored to death. In so many cases, people come to church expecting little to happen, and they are not disappointed.

The secret of an inspiring worship service is spontaneity. Whatever else is to be said about those "miracle-working" evangelists who feast off the desperate and the curious, at least it must be admitted that they keep their audiences guessing. Worship is by nature a devotional experience. Structure is valid as it provides for expression of the emotions, but invalid when it usurps spontaneity. Formality may serve those feelings which members of the congregation share in common. However, only informality can serve those feelings which are distinctively individual.

When the Asbury revival was sweeping the country in 1970, I went to conduct evangelistic services in a certain church which had planned three years for my coming. It so happened that the day before I was to arrive, a lay-witness team from a neighboring city had come to conduct the Sunday morning worship service. There was a great moving of the Holy Spirit upon the congregation that day, with several conversions and almost the whole church stirred.

Great excitement filled the air on the first night of our crusade Monday evening. Pews were filled early. A guest song director had been called and did a superb job of leading us in worship. I preached the sermon which I had carefully prepared. To our chagrin the service seemed utterly sterile. No one appeared to be moved. Why? We knew the answer. We had planned *too well*. The remainder of the week we met as the Quakers used to. Each service was unique and spontaneous. The results were surprising. The services were inspiring and attendance remained high. I learned that week that if someone wants to tamper with the roof, he may very well be in the will of the Lord.

We gather together to sense the Spirit of God moving upon the face of the deep. We want God to do it again. We want to witness another creation. We want there to be light. We want to see the Lord's handiwork and be so enthralled that we must agree, "It is good." What excites us more than to see sinners repent, the sick take up their beds and walk, the disconsolant filled with joy, and those who have been estranged come together?

Was not the appeal of the New Testament church its utter unpredictability? It may have been less than perfect, but dull and routine it wasn't. At times, people were converted by the thousands. People were filled with the Holy Spirit. The afflicted were healed of all manner of diseases. Ananias and Sapphira and also Simon were disciplined for ungodly attitudes. On one occasion the place where the believers were assembled was filled with the sound of a mighty rushing wind. Another time the place of meeting was shaken as by an earthquake following prayer. What was the result of all this? "And the word of God increased; and the number of the disciples multiplied greatly in Jerusalem" (Acts 6:7).

When worship is a "happening," crowds appear. The church today is in need of a new rumor. The old one is that worship is dead. Let the word go forth that Jesus is in the house, and things are lively.

[1]Helmut Thielicke, Trans. John W. Doberstein, *The Trouble with the Church* (New York: Harper and Row, 1965), p. viii.
[2]*The Trouble with the Church,* op. cit., p. viii.
[3]Elton Trueblood, *The Incendiary Fellowship* (New York: Harper and Row, 1967), p. 48.
[4]Wallace Fisher, *Preaching and Parish Renewal* (New York: Abingdon Press, 1966), p. 32.
[5]Merrill R. Abbey, *Preaching to the Contemporary Mind* (New York: Abingdon Press, 1963), p. 35.
[6]P. T. Forsyth, *Positive Preaching and the Modern Mind* (Cincinnati: Jennings and Graham, 1907), p. 81.

12

Happiness Is Helping

*Blessed is the church
whose mission is worldwide,
for her fruitfulness will be multiplied.*

Recently a young professional man shared with me his heartache regarding the plight of the local congregation with which he worships. Holding an earned doctor's degree and being a thoroughly dedicated Christian, he is bothered by what he considers both the church's ineptitude and its lethargy. He feels—with apparent good reason—that his local congregation is neither knowledgeable of nor concerned about the worldwide ministry of the communion of which it is a part.

This brilliant man labeled his pastor's sermons frightfully dull and platitudinal (while praising the man's personal uprightness). Little is ever done, reportedly, to improve the Christian education program. After many a Wednesday evening Bible study, which he considers fragmented, shallow, and irrelevant, he leaves the church asking himself, "Was it worth the effort to come?"

If we can believe that things are as bad as stated, here we have a picture of a church that knows little of what it means to be contemporary or mission-oriented. Unhappiness on the part of one (or more) of its most capable and loyal supporters is the result.

Unfortunately, there are those who would send the church out to save the world in a Model T and high-button shoes. Small wonder that young people and keen-minded adults are asking a crucial question, "Is the church relevant in our time?" There is no easy answer. It may or may not be. Everything depends upon the concept of ministry held by any given local congregation.

This does not mean the church should rush into every project called mission. The congregation which finds itself behind the times and needing to revolutionize its ministry, should first be clear on its priorities. Certainly change for the sake of change is no virtue, and this is what we appear to see in some places. The church of Jesus Christ must not in the name of relevancy feel obliged to hop on every bandwagon.

There is, it seems to me, too much faddism in the so-called new mission of the church. I recall a young man, now out of the ministry, who left an unhappy church in the wake of each of his moves. I think it was because, despite being utterly sincere and dedicated, he was always out in left field addressing the grandstands about his latest innovation while his congregation huddled around the pitcher's mound wondering how they were going to get the devil out.

Bishop Gerald Kennedy wrote a few years ago, "There is an insatiable hunger in some men for the new as an end in itself. They do not succeed in building the church, but they are experts at tearing down the old. They may experience a certain destructive exhilaration, but they are not the real servants of the church."[1]

The discerning church will be able to distinguish between sand and salt. Its people will be helped in this by the pastor who has a deft awareness of the idea whose time has come, but who does not believe that about every idea presented. While the traditionalist is no more relevant than the Pharisee praying on the street corner, those with an overactive social thyroid are no more relevant than was Martha's excessive concern over cooking when she should have been learning from Jesus.

In the latter case the problem seems to be that some, out of pure motive and in the face of dire need, give a cup of cold water in the Master's name. In doing so, they find such joy in alleviating misery that they insist the only right thing to do is give all the rest of us a dipper and send us out in search of thirsty people. That this is a misplaced zeal there should be little argument. That which is relevant in the relative is not necessarily relevant in the absolute.

Still, there are many things about which we cannot but be troubled. The church must be faithful in small things as well as large, if indeed, caring for the mental health, physical well-being, and social equality of men can be called small things. Hence, the concerned church will display and implement a social concern.

Jesus knew there was a time and a place to heal the sick, defend the oppressed, and speak out against injustices inflicted by the existing power structure. The church cannot keep the most sensitive souls among its fellowship if they are taught—either by precept or example—to pass by on the other side, while on every hand they see those who have fallen among thieves and to whom ministry is worthy, in the name of the Lord. If such ministry is not esteemed in the church, it will find its way outside the church, there to be used of the Lord and to receive his endorsement as did the anonymous servant who cast out demons in Jesus' name despite not following the twelve. No cause is so holy that it can afford to ignore secular needs. Even a burden for souls should at times yield to being touched with feelings of infirmities other than spiritual.

James Massey said it well in addressing an Anderson College chapel service, "The mandate of the gospel is not narrowed to concerns of the end-time alone. Mundane affairs demand a morality. . . . Life in this world is no one-sided issue. A vital and balanced theology will involve a social philosophy."

Led by a generation of youth who are offended by the selfish use of affluence, penalized by sins and miscalculations of the past, enlightened by unprecedented educational advantages, sensitized by the news media, driven by restless energy, threatened by oppressive conditions, and challenged by almost limitless opportunities, a new era of concern has dawned upon us.

Like it or not, this spirit has infected the church. Some resent it as the Pharisees did the world upsetting antics of the disciples. Others, wiser and more magnanimous, would caution, Gamaliel-like, "Let it alone for if it is not of God it will perish of itself; if it is of God there will be no stopping it and to try would be to fight against God." Others will tell you that if they are made to hold their peace, the very stones will cry out.

The relevant church will be predominately of the third persuasion. This is no time to argue about who will be the drum major. Who cares where the impetus comes from? This is a time to join the march, not the march of dissent or protest, but the parade of caring persons who are going about doing good everywhere.

The other morning my associate and I were crossing the Ohio River between Louisville, Kentucky, and Jeffersonville, Indiana. Suddenly, there on the bridge just ahead of us, a small van spun on the ice and whirled dizzily out of control. Helplessly we watched it crash head on into the iron lattice of the bridge. I stopped the car and we ran to the scene. The windshield of the truck had been broken out. The driver was draped over the steering wheel in a

101

dazed condition. Blood gushed from his forehead. John whipped out his handkerchief, gave it to the victim, and said, "Hold it to your head real hard."

The police were called while I redirected traffic and John stayed by the driver to offer moral support. When finally the man had been taken to the hospital and the wrecked truck hauled away, we continued on our way home, still shaken over the sight we had seen and the adventure in which we had taken part. Struck by a moment of self-awareness John mused, "I lost a monogrammed handkerchief in that deal."

"Well," I responded, "That's the cost of involvement." Both of us agreed it was a ridiculously small cost. Others have paid much more. The point is, we didn't reject the idea of helping just because it wasn't the work of a church committee or because it might have as easily been done by a hippie or commie.

On the day of this writing, I went home at lunch and found my wife talking on the telephone to the Bureau of Internal Revenue. She asked under what conditions a divorced woman might claim her children as income tax deductions. Further investigation revealed that much of her morning had been spent talking on the telephone, trying to help a young mother find her way through the maze of divorce proceedings.

The husband was making things as difficult as possible, and the wife, in her childlike helplessness had not known where to turn except to her friend in Christ, my wife. I am sure there are those in the church who would tell you that the pastor's wife might better have spent her morning tending to her business as president of the women's society. With all due respects to women's groups, I doubt it, for this too is the Lord's work.

Actually, my wife placed herself in little jeopardy, for ours is a caring congregation. Our people find their happiness, as well as their greatness, in service. Not long ago one of the men of our church spent a time of crisis in the hospital. Hardly had he arrived back home in the country than the pump on the well stopped. Ordinarily, it would have been a small matter for this strapping fellow to fix it. But here he was scarcely able to be out of bed. Word got around to certain men of the church. The old pump was found to be irreparable. The men bought and installed a new one in less time than a serviceman would have done it. It is hard to say who was happiest, those who gave or those who received.

One of the elderly men in our church is an outpatient at Jewish Hospital in Louisville. Daily he must be taken to the hospital for radium treatments for a malignancy which threatens his life. On their own initiative, men of our Brotherhood organized a transportation committee to chauffeur this man to the hospital and back home.

This same men's group participated in a civic project aimed at improving sublevel housing in our city. An elderly widow, whose humble dwelling received quite a face-lifting at the hands of our men, wrote, "I feel that I have seen true Christianity actually at work in modern dress. Sometimes, even at night now, I go outside and look up to make sure I didn't dream it all and that my pretty silver roof is still up there. Please know that I thank you every time it storms—and when the winter winds blow a gale, I'll think of you." Best of all, the "foreman" of the job developed a real friendship with this lonely individual and frequently stops to see her, even though officially the project has been over for quite some time.

One of the real unsung heroes among us is a registered nurse. Employed by a general practitioner, she literally takes her work home with her. She went faithfully to the home of a young mother suffering from terminal cancer, bathing the woman and otherwise performing professional

103

services on a volunteer basis. When the woman passed away, this nurse influenced her sorority to make a generous contribution to the family which was left with staggering medical bills.

On another occasion this same nurse paid for a black patient's out-patient treatment at the hospital, and even drove the woman to and from the hospital. The full extent of her helpfulness will never be known since what we know has been revealed quite incidentally. You might suspect that the nurse is an elderly woman, perhaps having no family and with an excess of time and money. Such is not the case. She is a young wife and mother with all the obligations this involves. She serves because she cares.

We hear many newspaper stories about those who "passed by on the other side," refusing to get involved in some critical situation. Certainly this does happen, but it is not characteristic of the people of congregations endued with Christ-like compassion. Other experiences that have brought us happiness as a congregation include: gifts distributed to residents of a nursing home at Christmas; visits to a children's hospital and an orphanage by our Senior High Youth; Thursday evening, one night a month, worship services conducted for years at the county home; an entire adult Sunday school class of some forty members holding their regular session at the county jail.

When Jesus washed the feet of his disciples, he taught us something very important about all forms of service, "Happy are ye if ye do them" (John 13:17). Every year during holy week, members of our congregation wash one another's feet. This is in keeping with the letter of Christ's commandment. Hopefully what we do the other fifty-one weeks is in keeping with the spirit of his lesson. At least our own joy tells us so.

---

[1]Gerald Kennedy, *With Singleness of Heart* (New York: Harper and Brothers, 1951), p. 45.

104

13

Happiness Is a Harvest

*Blessed is the church
where new births occur often,
for her family shall greatly increase.*

The happiest experiences in the Huttenlocker household have been those two occasions when increases came to our family. How my wife and I did rejoice when on March 2, 1956 a son was born to us, and again on January 30, 1962 when another boy arrived.

Nothing could be more natural than rejoicing over an enlarged family circle. Our experience certainly has not been unique. Each new member of the family means another life to whom we can give love and from whom we can receive love. The whole creation stems from our heavenly Father's very own desire to share relationships with other living souls. This is exemplified in the Garden of Eden.

The same principle applies to the church. The family of God is never happier than when new members are added. The church knows no greater morale booster than a birth announcement. Every time a Nicodemus comes to Jesus, if God's people know anything about it, there is great rejoicing.

Paul and Barnabas had been commissioned as missionaries and went forth with great success evangelizing the Gentiles. Conversions, in fact, were of such great numbers that it became necessary to inform the church in Jerusalem just exactly what was happening out there on the mission field. Paul and Barnabas took a furlough. As they journeyed to the council meeting, they visited Phenice and Samaria. There in Christian assemblies they reported the results of their labors (not unlike missionaries do today). This news "caused great joy to all the brethren" (Acts 15:3).

We are told that the angels in heaven rejoice over one soul that repents. In this they are exceeded by the church. Angels can only observe each blessed event, but God's people may actually assist in the process. Samuel Wolcott said it well when he wrote: "Christ for the world we sing; the world to Christ we bring, with joyful song: the newborn souls whose days, reclaimed from error's ways, inspired with hope and praise, to Christ belong."

The vital church *thinks* evangelistically. The great preoccupation of its people is with reaching out and bringing others to Christ. Soul winning is preeminent in the talk of the church, whether in formal planning or in informal conversation.

One of Frances Gardner Hunter's favorite stories has to do with a phone call she made home one evening while away on a speaking engagement. There was great enthusiasm as the family brought her up to date on the exciting Sunday morning service, what the pastor had said, who had received Christ, how many attended, and other details of a spiritual nature.

When it seemed that everything about the Lord's work had been recounted, Frances' teen-aged daughter added, almost as an afterthought, "Oh, by the way, mom, Tom's new Corvette was stolen, and police haven't been able to find a trace of it." (Tom is Mrs. Hunter's son.) Frances says, "This really grabbed me, because their vital Christianity made it necessary to tell me about Christian activities first." Once people experience the joy of sharing Christ, secular interests always finish a poor second.

If conversions are to occur with regularity it is absolutely essential that evangelism becomes a congregation's way of life. It has to be in the forefront of everyone's thinking, not a subconscious or subsidiary ambition, but the number one thing, the reason for which the fellowship exists.

I once spent a week as the guest of a Christian businessman. I accompanied him on several occasions as he went about his work. Business was his topic of conversation from the time he arose in the morning until he retired in the evening. It was easy for me to tell where his heart was. With much apparent satisfaction he spoke of the deals he had completed in the past, those presently being consummated, and others which he contemplated closing in the future. Perhaps it took that singleness of purpose to bring him success. Certainly he had done well. This is the sort of wholehearted devotion found among those most successful in bringing others to Christ. They too are obsessed with a purpose.

It is not surprising that some churches seldom see conversions in their midst. While this businessman—thoroughly schooled in evangelical theology and supposedly himself a product of the born-again way—was doing well for himself, he was utterly failing Christ. He was neglecting his first responsibility as a Christian: that of witnessing.

When a majority of those within a congregation become preoccupied with their own private affairs, evangelism inevitably suffers. Outreach breaks down. The aim of the church is not refuted. It is simply brushed aside. Soul winning becomes the other fellow's business. Thus the church is the victim of a corrosive, secularizing process.

There is little hope that any church will find joy apart from a passion for souls. The congregation whose fellowship has become listless, impersonal, perhaps even ill-tempered, can best be transformed by a new mind-set, the same one which motivated Paul and Barnabas.

During a series of evangelistic services in a southern church, a group of concerned young wives decided they should get together to consider how they might more effectively share Christ with their friends. I was invited to their delicious potluck lunch. These were cultured women whose husbands held high-salaried positions. After we finished eating we had a very stimulating around-the-table discussion about personal witnessing. It was a refreshing departure from the trivia so often heard by evangelists around dinner tables. I firmly believe that great good resulted from that meeting.

The dynamic church *functions* evangelistically. Talk turns to action once the fellowship disperses. A great invasion force is turned loose on the community. Everyday situations become the context for presentation of the gospel.

What Christians say about Christ through the week largely determines what the world does about him on Sunday. The congregation which sings about Christ during its worship but then becomes silent about Christ in its confrontation with a pagan society resembles a business which has a great amount of interoffice communication, but no salesmen out on the field.

A man once said to his pastor, "Don't talk to me about personal soul winning. I don't want any part of it. It simply isn't my thing." Then he attended one of those informal evangelistic services which spread over the country during the Asbury revival in 1970. The inspiration of that service completely changed his mind. He saw firsthand what happens to a congregation when great numbers of its people overcome their inhibitions and let the glory of Christ shine through them. The next night he was primed and ready as he reported for the second shift at the factory where he worked. By midnight he had shared the Four Spiritual Laws (Campus Crusade) with six different fellow workers.

One congregation is the salt of the earth. Another is taken with a grain of salt. What is the difference? The former moves out boldly into the world to make Christ known. The latter shrivels timidly within its own confines. One takes seriously the Great Commission. The other only pretends to. One is a radiant church. The other casts about for a source of joy.

Only as believers use every opportunity to witness does the world "take note that they have been with Jesus." It seems that some of us have borrowed from the film makers an idea by which we rate our testimonies. They are for some audiences, but not for others. In an inverted way we have thus made our Lord's name an undesirable word. The intimation is that speaking of Christ makes a person guilty of great indiscretion. Nothing stifles the progress of a church quicker than for that kind of heresy to spread throughout the fellowship.

Ethel Waters said recently on one of the network TV talk shows, "Honey, when I get a chance to say a good word for Jesus, that's my thing." The problem in many congregations is that saying a good word for Jesus is just not the thing of enough people.

The joy of reaping cannot be separated from the joy of sowing. We need to convince ourselves that it is a pleasure to share Christ, rather than limiting our joy to those times when we ride the coattails of someone else's faithful witness. As is our experience of joy, so shall be our expression of it. Jesus said, "For out of the abundance of the heart the mouth speaketh" (Matt. 12:34). Perhaps if we had more of the abundance of his grace, we would find it easier to glorify him.

A college professor and a Christian psychologist were discussing the matter of communicating one's pleasure in serving Christ. Said the professor, "I find it a joy to witness to my fellow faculty members. Some of them look at me like I must be joking. To me religion is exciting and joyous."[1]

Members of the vital church are only incidentally concerned about how they appear to others. Their primary concern is to afford all who meet them an opportunity to know and enjoy Christ as they do.

Any church will thrive on evangelism. Additions to the family not only make the church happy, they also make it hardy. The gates of hell turn aside from the congregation whose ranks steadily swell. Satan finds it difficult (if not impossible) to spread discord, lethargy, or apostasy when "the Lord adds to the church daily such as should be saved" (Acts 2:47). His every subversive tactic is trampled beneath the cadenced march of the church.

A certain church had been torn by pettiness and strife over the years. But then a revival broke out in that congregation, beginning with the conversion of one or two persons for whom a number of the people had earnestly prayed over a period of time. Soon hearts began to melt. Faults were confessed. Repentance was widespread. Suddenly, no one felt that having his or her own way was nearly so important as furthering the church's ministry in that community. Thus has revival cured the ills of many a congregation.

110

Only those who have participated in a pentecost can fully understand the joy that goes with it. There is contentment and a sense of fulfillment which know no counterpart in sensual pleasure.

More than once I have driven home after preaching in a series of evangelistic meetings and been almost oblivious to the world around me. There was the time in northeast Ohio when the final service had been an especially fitting climax to a wonderful week. The lights of the city faded into the background and the darkness of the countryside enveloped me.

Alone with my thoughts, and reliving the ecstacy of past adventure, I became lost in wonder, love, and praise. Before I knew it I had missed a fairly familiar turn and found myself off course. Although I had to drive several miles out of the way and was later than expected in arriving home, it didn't matter. My joy was only so much the longer preserved.

If the church will conscientiously "weep o'er the erring one" and "lift up the fallen," she shall harvest her reward. A congregation having a sense of purpose with an accompanying sense of achievement cannot but be contented. The ministry of both pastor and people will be self-authenticating. What the church today needs as much as anything else is a restoration of confidence. The church has been maligned for its hypocrisy, irrelevance, incompetence, and failure. What we need is a success story to build up our sagging ego.

Nothing helps the church affirm its primacy in God's plan like a landslide of conversions. If the church can point to lives that have been changed, it most eloquently defends its appointment, illuminates its contribution, and asserts its indestructibility.

"BE-ATTITUDES" FOR THE CHURCH

The discouragements of a first pastorate remain vividly with me. There was but a handful of faithful Christians. We were so handicapped: limited in facilities, funds, and resources. There were times when I nearly despaired of our future in that place. It was not an easy community in which to evangelize (is there such a place?). But then we would arrange for a series of revival meetings. The saints would begin to pray with new enthusiasm and hope. The evangelist would come to us prepared and eager to give his best. Soon things would begin to happen.

One unusual man of God especially endeared himself to all of us. A former Salvation Army Captain, night after night he recounted heart-warming salvation experiences of former sinners. A number of persons sought spiritual help that week and much lasting good was done. We thanked God and again took heart.

The story of the vital church has no finish. It cannot end so long as God's family keeps increasing. Luke's description of that dynamic fellowship of the New Testament era says simply that they continued praising God and having favor with all the people. May it be true of every congregation on earth.

------

[1]R. Lofton Hudson, *Helping Each Other Be Human* (Waco, Texas: Word Books, 1970), p. 40.